OTHERWORLDLY
ENCOUNTERS

About the Author

Nomar Slevik (Bangor, Maine) is a ufologist and paranormal researcher. He is a member of Paranormal Research in Maine (P.R.I.ME Paranormal).

To Write the Author

If you wish to contact the author or would like more information about this book, please write to the author in care of Llewellyn Worldwide, and we will forward your request. Both the author and publisher appreciate hearing from you and learning of your enjoyment of this book and how it has helped you. Llewellyn Worldwide cannot guarantee that every letter written to the author can be answered, but all will be forwarded. Please write to:

Nomar Slevik
⅍ Llewellyn Worldwide
2143 Wooddale Drive
Woodbury, MN 55125-2989

Please enclose a self-addressed stamped envelope for reply,
or $1.00 to cover costs. If outside the USA, enclose
an international postal reply coupon.

NOMAR SLEVIK

OTHERWORLDLY ENCOUNTERS

EVIDENCE

OF

UFO SIGHTINGS

AND

ABDUCTIONS

Llewellyn Worldwide
Woodbury, Minnesota

FIRST EDITION
First Printing, 2018

Book design by Bob Gaul
Cover design by Kevin R. Brown
Editing by Sandy Sullivan
Interior photos supplied by author except page 88 by the Library of Congress, page 101 by Robert Osbourne, pages 124–25, 127–28 by MUFON and pages 234–35 by Loring Air Force Base

Llewellyn Publications is a registered trademark of Llewellyn Worldwide Ltd.

Library of Congress Cataloging-in-Publication Data (Pending)
ISBN: 978-0-7387-5715-5

Llewellyn Publications
A Division of Llewellyn Worldwide Ltd.
2143 Wooddale Drive
Woodbury, MN 55125-2989
www.llewellyn.com

Printed in the United States of America

This book is dedicated to the love of my life, April.
You are the reason that I enjoy every single day.
Thank you for supporting (putting up with?)
my strange passion. You are my mainstay,
you are the safe harbor I so desperately need.

CONTENTS

"Spectres from heaven are rational creatures, and come down from the fountain of reason, and will therefore deal reasonably with us, by allowing us a fair opportunity to ascertain the reality of their mission. But for this examination, the mind is incapable when terrified by a sudden surprise."

—Reverend Abraham Cummings, 1859

ACKNOWLEDGMENTS

First, I must thank all the people who have reported their encounters. Without you, there would be nothing to research or investigate, and friendships would have been missed. Second, my publisher and editor, thank you! You have made my UFO obsession turn into authorship once again. Third, my ragtag team of researchers, writers, and UFO maniac friends who share this passion and with whom I've had some great conversations: Erik Cooley, Valerie Schultz, Joe Kelly, Josh Powers, Jason Merritt, Brian Thompson, and Kyle Sawyer.

I'd like to thank those who inspired the need to research, investigate, and write about this topic: Stanton Friedman, Loren Coleman, Jenny Randles, Charles Fort, Linda Godfrey, Jason Hawes, Josh Gates, and Michelle Souliere.

And lastly, to my family. I would like to thank my parents and sister and her family for their continued support. And to April and Malik, you make everything better.

FOREWORD

By Martin Willis

Being immersed in the area that you are writing about is an advantage for authors who write about incidents of UFO sightings. You know more about what the people in that area are like; you know their everyday lives, nuances, and how to approach them. Growing up in Maine, and spending most of my life here after living just over fifteen years combined in Colorado and California, I have come to realize Mainers are a special breed. We deal with tough winters, hard work, and summers full of tourists with their own ideas on what Maine is or isn't. I find that when a Mainer looks you in the eye and tells you a story in earnest, for the most part you can count on the authenticity of it.

I grew up in the small town of Eliot, about 2,500 people, which is featured in one of this book's chapters ("Village of the Strange"). I left for Colorado two years prior to the incident Nomar writes about, but I am almost certain I would know the witness by his full, real name. During the 1960s, there was a lot of talk about UFOs in the area, especially at school recess or sometimes even in the classroom. I remember hearing of alleged sightings, but nothing concrete. However, as the flap about area sightings grew, there was a hoax created by some teenagers with lights and dirt bikes out in a local gravel pit.

It took many years and an actual sighting of my own to take a hard look at the UFO topic. I was in Carmel Valley, California, in 2006 at dusk and watched a perfectly shaped disk move overhead, stop, and move again without a sound. Ridiculed while trying to report it to the police department and again at my workplace for describing it, I decided that going forward, I would keep the encounter to myself. It wasn't until I moved back to Maine in 2011 that I started taking a serious look at UFOs again and wondered why there was any ridicule at all. During my own research, I have found countless stories by credible, intelligent people who have witnessed something unknown in our skies. The more I talk to these people about their encounters, the further I get from understanding what or who these encounters are with. It has been an interesting ride.

After starting a podcast (*Podcast UFO*) shortly after I landed in Maine, I began wondering about local Maine encounters. I had recalled hearing about the Allagash Abductions, but not much else other than the stories from my home town. In 2014, I heard of a book being published, *UFOs Over Maine: Close Encounters from the Pine Tree State.* It was exciting that there was finally a book where I could read about encounters from my own state, and I thoroughly enjoyed Nomar Slevik's writing style.

With his new work, *Otherworldly Encounters: Evidence of UFO Sightings and Abductions,* Nomar has dug deep into brand new or often recounted Maine sightings to share fascinating cases, ones sure to keep you on the edge of your seat. This book is highly engaging and contains some spine-tingling UFO and abduction cases. Also, the way in which Nomar writes about his own investigations is nothing short of fascinating. He has conducted personal interviews with witnesses, dived headfirst into declassified Project Blue Book files, and brought forth newly discovered information that has never been in print (such as Mothman in Maine, a man abducted from Bangor who fought his alien captors and lived to tell the tale, and truly bizarre encounters reported from Dow Air Force Base). Being a fan of history, I found the chapters "Nineteenth-Century UFOs," "Escape to Witch Mountain," and "The Psychic Who Saved the World" utterly captivating.

The encounters this book dissects are totally engrossing, especially with the array of clearly documented statements from witnesses. *Otherworldly Encounters: Evidence of UFO Sightings and Abductions* is a wholly successful contribution to the cultural debate about UFO phenomena that will inspire and encourage others in researching cases, and witnesses in reporting their encounters, well into the future.

—Sebago, Maine
April 4, 2017

INTRODUCTION

This book serves to bring to light encounters of unexplained phenomena. Included are UFOs, men in black, crop circles, alien abductions, monsters, extraterrestrial biological entities, werewolves, balls of light, Mothman, and more. There are stories about lights in the sky and aliens on the ground (whoa!). There are reports dating back to the 1800s, tales of landed UFOs and of military witnesses, and my personal investigations from around the state.

The accomplishment of publishing my first book, *UFOs Over Maine*, established my reputation locally as a credible investigator. I say this because when I reached out to witnesses, organizations, and police departments while researching this new work, more people got back to me wanting their stories to be told. In some cases, I was allowed to use their names; in others, I have used pseudonyms.

Many of the tales are straightforward and factual; in several others, I have enhanced the bare-bones report with creative dialogue and my interpretation of the scene. My research, always earnest in its approach, took on a life of its own, and the burden became which stories to include, so as not to send my publisher a five-hundred-page draft.

The way in which I approach investigations differs somewhat from popular methods in ufology, as I also pull from my background as a paranormal investigator. I don't just simply interview a witness—I get to know them and have genuine conversations. I go on-site to where the encounter occurred and immerse myself in the environment as much as possible. In doing so, I can get a sense of the area and of what the witness felt, and I can capture any possible evidence with the gear from my paranormal bag of tricks. This includes EMF detectors, night vision cameras, digital audio recorders, full-spectrum cameras, and parabolic microphones, to name a few. Also, some of the witnesses I interviewed reached out to me directly via email and Facebook to share their stories, some of which are in this book. Pretty cool!

In this book, I have brought in Valerie Schultz, the State Director for the Mutual UFO Network (MUFON) in Maine. MUFON was created in 1969 in order to investigate the UFO phenomena. Roger Marsh, MUFON's Director of Communications, offered this description of the organization for my first book: "Today, MUFON continues to grow internationally and is the largest and most recognized UFO organization in the world. MUFON has a State Director in each of the fifty states and thirty-six National Directors internationally, as well as over a thousand Field Investigators worldwide." As Valerie points out in her essay below, MUFON's mission statement is "the Scientific Study of UFOs for the Benefit of Humanity." Valerie has contributed greatly to this book and coauthored some of the stories you will read later ("Invasion in Scarborough" and "Starship Trooper," just to name a couple).

I also brought in Erik Cooley, friend and fellow UFO enthusiast. In some cases, Erik assisted in research and contacting witnesses for interviews. He also coauthored the stories "Trappers in Athens" and "The Dark Skies of Orrington." He has a fresh perspective on ufology and, like Valerie, shares his thoughts below.

As you already know from the foreword, I asked my friend and UFO podcaster Martin Willis if he would share his thoughts on the UFO phenomenon. He has a comprehensive approach to the topic that I feel garners attention.

Lastly, I enjoy including my own encounters, personal investigations, and lessons learned as a way to establish a foundation. This also serves as an outlet for my thoughts on life and candidly shows my passion for the subject matter. So I ask you to follow me on this journey through the woods, lakes, farms, and towns of Maine. It is an interesting one and I am so excited to share it with all of you. Thank you for your continued support, and look up! You never know what you may see.

UFOs and MUFON

By Valerie Schultz, MUFON State Director for Maine

The thought of extraterrestrial life has always fascinated me! As a child, I spent many evenings enjoying the night sky. I loved astronomy, so finding the Big Dipper, Orion, Venus, and Jupiter and following the phases of the moon were a source of joy. On those clear and star-filled nights I always found myself imagining what life might be like on other worlds. With the vastness of our universe it just seemed natural to me that there was life out there. I thought someday in the future we would know for sure and possibly discover that life comes in many forms. However, even today there is so much that we don't know or comprehend. Perhaps there are portals on this planet where extraterrestrials can come and go from other dimensions. Could there be time travelers that visit Earth from the future? Is it possible that there are civilizations out there that can harness the energy from the elements of the universe and travel extremely long distances? These are just some of my thoughts that could be proven true through scientific verification soon.

The great sci-fi movies of the 1950s fueled my imagination at a young age. *The Day the Earth Stood Still* focused on the mistrust and reaction of humanity to alien contact. Unfortunately, all these years later, I'm sorry to say that I believe the reaction would be similar if it occurred today. Even so, it is still one of my favorite sci-fi movies!

I remember reading many Frank Edwards books as a youngster, such as *Flying Saucers—Serious Business* and *Stranger Than Science*. They were my first exposure to events that could not be explained. Erich von Däniken's *Chariots of the Gods? Unsolved Mysteries of the Past* was a monumental work that influenced my thinking. It opened my eyes to the possibility that Earth had been visited repeatedly by advanced beings. By examining ancient ruins and lost civilizations, Mr. Von Däniken raised questions about our history. His book gave me a great deal to consider and taught me how to think outside of the box.

In the 1980s I was a member of John Keel's Fortean Society in New York City. He had very interesting guests that spoke at his monthly meetings, such as Whitley Streiber, Tim Beckley, and Antonio Huneeus. It was these Fortean Society meetings that really inspired me to get into studying UFOs. I then discovered and followed the works of Stanton Friedman, a nuclear physicist and outstanding pioneer in the field of ufology. He was the original civilian investigator of the Roswell Incident and I became fascinated with his research, which led me on a path to MUFON to learn more about the UFO phenomenon.

I joined MUFON in 2010, and soon after studied and passed the exam to become a MUFON Field Investigator. It has been an honor to conduct UFO investigations on behalf of this organization. I became the Maine Assistant State Director in 2012 and am currently the Maine State Director.

MUFON is dedicated to "the Scientific Study of UFOs for the Benefit of Humanity." We are the oldest UFO organization in the world, and since 1969 we have grown to 4,000 members with more than 800 Certified Investigators. When a sighting is reported to MUFON, it is given a case number and a trained investigator will then be assigned to interview the witness and follow up on the report. We also have an Experiencer Research Team, a Nationwide Rapid Response Team, and a Special Assignment Team who stand ready to assist when needed. MUFON takes UFO sightings seriously. Our investigators are all volunteers who gladly give their time to assist in discovering what the UFO phenomenon is all about. One of our goals is to educate the public on the UFO phenomenon. Our History Channel show *Hangar 1: The UFO Files* was one method of achieving that goal. Another is our monthly *MUFON UFO Journal*, which is available to members.

Maine MUFON receives several sighting reports per month. It is said that per capita, Maine receives the third highest number of sightings out of all the states. We have received some very intriguing sightings over the last few years, and through this book, Maine MUFON is pleased to share some of them with the public. You'll read about a UFO sighting at a drive-in theater in Scarborough, a possible abduction in Athens, a crop circle, disc-shaped craft, and possible men in black in Union. There are stories about three pulsating thirty-foot orbs that resembled volcanic lava as they moved above the runway at Dow Air Force Base in Bangor, and a huge silent craft that recently traveled over southern Maine and made witnesses ill as they observed it. Nomar Slevik's first book, *UFOs Over Maine: Close Encounters from the Pine Tree State*, was an informative, thought-provoking, and very enjoyable read. Now, with *Otherworldly Encounters: Evidence of UFO Sightings and Abductions*, Nomar will take you further on his journey through the unusual, bizarre, and unexplained events that have occurred past and present throughout our great state! Enjoy!

One Man's Quest for the Truth
By Erik Cooley

Why ufology? Sometimes the idea of the unknown is much more interesting than the ordinary. As a society, we focus so much on what we know rather than what we could know. The concept that we humans could possibly be the only entity in all the universes and spaces of time seems ludicrous; if we exist, then why not others? It seems a narcissistic concept that we are the only ones privileged to have an existence. I truly believe there is more in the universe than just the Earth and we who live on it. Could my belief just be resistance to conformity, since I have always had a questionable outlook on the norm or the expected? Am I a conspiracy theorist? I don't believe so; based upon my life experiences and what I have learned from others, I find that looking beyond face value is worth the effort.

People have long tried to point to ufologists as being eccentric and unstable, and much like with politicians, cases of the extreme tend to exaggerate the sample size. Have I ever experienced a UFO? No, I have not, and with this admission I may be sacrificing credibility, but I see the subject as someone who is an unbiased examiner of the evidence. Before I gained an interest in UFOs and the possible existence of aliens, I was always intrigued by cases of the unknown, whether it was a national murder case or a local missing persons report. I remember the first time I sat down with someone and listened openly to the concept of UFOs and the possibility that we are not alone in this universe. I remember being fascinated by that thought, and with story after story, I couldn't help but feel excited that there had to be more to this topic than we are led to believe.

After hearing the stories from John Keel about Mothman, the Allagash Abductions, and the Loring Air Force Base encounters, I became instantly captivated by what was missing—the truth. You see, the thing about UFO sightings is that they are almost instantly rebuffed by skeptics and even by our own government. But how could all these sightings and examples be false? And how could there always have been some reason why it could not have happened, rather than why it could? I want to delve more into this. We hope you find these stories just as fascinating as we did.

"The supernatural is only a step away from the world we sometimes arrogantly describe as 'real.'"

—C. J. Stevens

ONLY A STEP AWAY

An old man with unkempt hair quietly crossed the street. He wore moon boots and a leather jacket with an American flag on the back. Once across the street, he looked up. He seemed tired, but not once did he look away. Slowly his hand rose to his mouth to cover the surprise on his face. Others walked by without giving the man a second thought. But I saw him. Not in some poetic *I notice the faceless people on the street* type of way. He captured my interest because he was seeing something that others weren't. And that, to me, was noteworthy. Was he lost in thought? What did he witness that stopped him dead in his tracks on a busy street corner in Boston, Massachusetts?

The year was 2008, and I was on a weekend getaway. I was also on the verge of moving to Bangor, Maine, after years of living in my favorite part of the state, Portland. I had lived in Boston for a bit after high school, and there were so many distractions that the paranormal didn't really have a place there—except for one night back in December of 1996.

That cold night in 1996, my roommate and I were out on the town to celebrate my birthday. Well, as much as two nineteen-year-olds could with only twenty dollars between them. Even though the night was young, we were broke and cold, so we made our way home. I was in an unfamiliar area of the city that my roommate knew better, so I followed him to the closest Green Line T-stop. As we walked, the atmosphere seemed to change. It was subtle, so I kept it to myself and continued walking. After a few minutes, my roommate said, "It's right up here" and gestured to the T-stop ahead. I looked where he was pointing, and noticed that we had just started walking through a new block that housed a massive office building. Most of the lights were off except for the top couple of floors. *Cleaners*, I thought, still unable to shake the ominous feeling I had.

We settled in on the T-stop bench and waited for our ride. My roommate noticed it first. "Look," he said, and pointed up toward the building. I looked at him and followed his index finger to a window near the top of the building. It was obvious what had caught his attention once I spotted it for myself. Someone stood in the window and stared down at us.

"Whoa," I whispered, unable to take my eyes off the figure. My roommate, after a long stare upward, said, "It's probably just some creep trying to freak us out." "I don't know, man," I said hesitantly. "It hasn't moved and it feels like it's staring into my friggin' soul." This resulted in an eruption of laughter, which was exactly what we both needed. "That was so lame!" my friend squeaked out in between laughs. The distraction broke my stare at the window, and when I looked back, whatever it was had disappeared.

What I found interesting, looking back on this incident years later, was that we had been in a large city but it felt like no one noticed us, nor we them. We had this experience in a very busy section of Boston, and the passersby seemed to melt away. There was only me, my roommate, and that building. I wonder if that's how that old man I saw in 2008 felt. No one noticed him stopped on that sidewalk staring at who-knows-what. Did he notice them? Or was he wrapped up in his own experience, just as I had been?

On that busy street corner, the old man continued to gaze. My gaze finally followed his, but I saw nothing. I kept looking for a moment until I was sure that I wasn't missing anything. When I looked back at the man, his gaze was now on the sidewalk and he was smiling. I couldn't help but smile, too. What had he seen? *A UFO?* I quickly thought, and did not dismiss it. Perhaps his smile was one of peace. Maybe he knew something that the rest of us didn't, so he smiled.

Silver Ball in the Bangor Sky

In the winter of 2007, I lived in Freeport, Maine, and worked for a wholesale auto parts company out of Portland. My job was to deliver various auto parts to mechanics from Portland to Bangor. During one of my trips up north, I was parked at a storage facility unloading a few items from my truck when a shiny object caught my eye. I turned my head and saw something in the sky that appeared to be hovering over Penobscot Bay. It was silver and round like a Christmas ornament. I stared at it for a few minutes, and then it vanished. There was no high-speed acceleration; it didn't even "blink out." It simply vanished; it was there, and then it was gone. I almost didn't notice at first. I stared at an empty sky until I realized it wasn't there anymore.

I kept looking at the sky, and I found myself smiling. Smiling like that old man. I think that incident is what keeps me gazing at the sky. Sure, I look up more often than most. I'm always trying to catch a glimpse of something, anything (a thunderbird would be awesome!). But that incident taught me that when you least expect it, something may be there. So, I look. When I drive, day or night, I look. When I have a cigarette break at work, or clean the snow off my car (it's winter in Maine as I write this, yikes!), I look. I've seen some interesting things just by paying attention, just by looking. Do I think everything I have seen is an extraterrestrial craft? Of course not. Some are shooting stars, some are meteors, some are satellites. But some, well, I don't know.

Two Ghosts and Two UFOs!

On a Friday afternoon in July of 2011, I traveled south from Bangor, headed to the state capital, Augusta. I was going to Franklin Street to conduct a paranormal investigation of a former bakery and the adjacent warehouse. I had been there numerous times previously with my paranormal investigation team, Paranormal Research in Maine (P.R.I.ME Paranormal), but on that night, it would be just me and the location's owner. Earlier in the week he'd reached out to me to discuss some of the recent paranormal encounters that he was experiencing. We'd discussed the possibility of my team coming back, but our schedules did not allow for this, so I offered to come down by myself for a bare-bones investigation. An investigation of this sort simply meant using minimal equipment and people. On that night, I brought a handheld night vision camcorder, a digital camera, a couple of K-IIs (EMF detectors), and some digital audio recorders.

Once on-site, the owner and I quickly exchanged pleasantries and got right down to the investigation. The location was a two-story brick building built in the early to mid twentieth century. The first floor served as the business area while the second floor was home to the original owner's family. The first floor now consisted of offices, a game room (billiards), a storage room complete with an embalming table (previously used by the bakery to wash pans and baking utensils, dang!), and a large room where several classic collectible automobiles were currently on display (car room).

A figure captured with night vision camera in a carport.

The floors appeared to be made of burnt pine, beautifully polished. The second floor (the living quarters) consist of multiple bedrooms, a living room area, a sunroom, a kitchen, a bathroom, and a laundry room. There were two sets of large stairs on either side of the warehouse, both leading to the basement. Additionally, there was a large patio area outside the laundry room where, during the time the bakery was in operation, parties were held. Finally, there was a full, unfinished basement consisting of a large open area and three smaller unfinished rooms. (At the time of this writing, the owner has finished the basement into a beautiful lounge area.)

While setting up in the area we wanted to investigate first, we discussed how we would conduct ourselves as "casually living and hanging about the property" much like the owner did daily, which had resulted in numerous paranormal encounters. An investigation done in this manner, in my opinion, would allow me a glimpse into the day-to-day activity that was experienced. Many times, the owner was at work in his office or in the "car room" on his laptop and would spy a shadow out of the corner of his eye, or sometimes, a picture hanging on the far corner of the room would suddenly fall off the wall.

We started the investigation in the "car room" by conducting a casual EVP session. Lights were kept on and we were conversational. Almost immediately, we started getting wraps and knocks in response to our questions. I had the K-II meter turned on, but no fluctuations in electric magnetic fields were detected during this active period. After a while, the responsive noises stopped, and we decided to move to the "billiards room." Numerous experiences had occurred there as well, witnessed by many friends and visitors to the home. Notably, while playing pool, witnesses had observed shadow movement from the hallway running perpendicular to the room. Laughter and coughs had been heard, and a marble moving on its own was captured on camera.

We settled in on a couch and chair on what looked like a staging area in the back of the room. There, we resumed our conversational EVP session. Some noises were heard in the room, some even responsive, but the momentum from the "car room" did not follow us. Our discussion moved away from the bakery and activity and we started having more personal conversations. We talked about work and UFOs, family and Bigfoot. After a little while, the owner noticed some shadow activity from the hallway at the far end of the room. I missed those movements and decided to focus my attention there. For a time, I observed nothing. Then, while we talked (he was relating a story from his childhood), I briefly looked toward the hallway. I saw something, but it wasn't a shadow.

I stood up and asked, "Did you see that?" "See what?" the owner replied. I told him that when I'd looked down at the hallway, I saw the last bit of a leg moving past the door- way. He assumed I saw a shadow, but I didn't. I saw a flesh and blood calf muscle and some white material toward the top of it; perhaps white shorts or a skirt. Upon hearing this, the owner explained that during the time the bakery was operational, male workers wore white shirts and pants, and the female workers wore knee-length white dresses. It was possible that I may have witnessed one of the female work- ers, and this excited us.

I walked the length of the room to the hallway, but saw nothing. The hallway felt cold, but the night was very humid and I'm sure my walk to the hallway had cooled my sweat to the point where I could confuse it with a cold spot. I observed no other activity in the hallway, so I resumed my perch on the couch.

After thirty minutes or so, we decided to move back to the "car room." We continued talking, though no further activity was observed, or so we thought. Suddenly, in the middle of our conversation, I noticed something behind the owner. My eyes shifted away from his and settled on the back portion of one of the vehicles on display. Standing there, seemingly leaning against the vehicle, I saw a shadow person. I could see the outline of a head and shoulders, and of a partial arm. It appeared the entity saw me notice it, since it darted off quickly to the left. As it did so, I saw its body turn to the left and I observed the elbow portion of its arm, as if it had turned and run away. The whole experience lasted only a few seconds, but it was quite exciting.

After another hour or so, the activity came to a complete stop. We parted ways, and I was satisfied with our organic approach to the investigation. We'd had great conversations and a few thrilling encounters. But as I was packing up my car and getting ready for my drive back to Bangor, a different type of encounter unexpectedly occurred.

With the car packed, I closed my trunk. As I did so, I looked up into the sky and saw a sparkling gold "thing" float slowly by. If I had to estimate its altitude, I would guess one hundred feet, when compared to the tall apartment buildings it passed by. It was silent and in constant motion, not keeping any identifiable shape. The only thing I could compare it to would be a child's sparkler attached to an arrow, shot with a bow into the air.

The event lasted no longer than twenty seconds, since the sparkling thing disappeared behind a building. I looked back at the building I had just investigated and contemplated if I should go and tell the owner what I had seen. But

I didn't. It was late, he already had the lights off, and I had a little over an hour to drive.

I swiftly navigated the side streets of Augusta and found Interstate 95 in about ten minutes. I put on a CD by the group Grand Buffet and cracked the driver's side window to have a smoke. As I made my way past the Waterville exits, the CD ended, so I turned on the radio and set my dial to *Coast to Coast AM*. George Noory was interviewing Dr. Paul Connett about the toxicity of fluoride when a red light, just above the tree tops, came into my field of vision. It traveled in a high arc from one side of the highway to the other, right to left. I know this may sound crazy, but it looked exactly like the other oddity I had spotted earlier that night. Again, it looked as though someone was behind the tree line on the right side of the highway and had shot a sparkler tied to an arrow toward the left side of the highway. This object traveled faster than the first one, which allowed for a brief observation, say ten seconds.

I quickly shut George Noory off and drove with my jaw dropped for a moment. I thought, *Well, what the hell was that?!* and wished I could rewind what I had just seen. I was wide awake for the rest of the drive and kept the radio off so I could concentrate. Both incidents were odd, no denying that, but what were they? It was July still; could people have been setting off fireworks? The first sighting had no sound. The second, well, I was driving with a window cracked and the radio on, so I have no idea if it made a sound. What I do know is that if it was fireworks, it did not burst into any sort of colored plume of sparks. It just went from one side of the highway to the other. Weird.

Perception

I have been on a lot of paranormal investigations and have seen some odd things in the sky. The one constant throughout every location, client, and experience is perception. Clients can embellish, locations can seem ominous, and experiences are nothing more than someone's perception, just like my "fireworks UFOs." But let's stop for a moment and think about that word, *perception*. According to Dictionary.com, in psychology it's defined as "a single unified awareness derived from sensory processes while a stimulus is present." The idea of perception can help us arrive at a better understanding of what the paranormal could really mean—not for our society today, but as a scientifically defined and universally accepted concept in a not-so-distant future.

Perception is different for all of us. It includes everything surrounding us; the makeup of our thoughts, actions, and personality; and how we conduct our lives and what we do with them. Perception is how we see the world, our loved ones, and friends. It's how we react to bumps in the night or lights in the sky. Case in point: In 1999, I gave my roommate a ride to work very early one morning. As this was their first day on the job, with no car, they had asked for a ride and I obliged. It was four o'clock in the morning while I drove. I started to sense a large object in the sky, and it seemingly loomed over my vehicle. The interior of the car started to glow and I slowly turned my head, ready for a close encounter.

Time slowed down, and my tired eyes found the source of the light. I looked on in disbelief… There, above us, hovered a UFO not forty feet away. Its lights illuminated the surrounding area. I panicked and turned to my roommate and said, "That's not good." I looked down the road, saw more lights headed toward us, and I'll tell you what, they looked like a fleet of starships, poised and ready for war.

Finally, my roommate responded calmly yet sarcastically, "Those are street lights, you idiot!" I snapped out of my sleep-deprived trance and looked at the large object again. Ah yes… perception… *Streetlight*, I thought, *I see you now.* Aware of my tenuous misjudgment and with resounding candor, I thanked the streetlight for the experience.

While not a paranormal event, the experience was most certainly noteworthy. It helped me to understand that perception is reality. Of course, I have always known this to be true, but as with most common things, it is not always at the forefront of your mind. It's terribly easy to fall prey to misperception and misidentification. When subtly at work in a situation, its impact can be profound. I say this because that has been my experience—rather, my perception. I was in a moment where I truly thought a UFO, an actual extraterrestrial vehicle, had closed in on my car, and I was frightened. When confronted with the reality of the situation, I felt a rush of relief. But that does not take away from the fact that for a moment, aliens existed, and I knew it to be true. It was my reality.

I take this knowledge with me on every investigation, with every client I interview, and two things occur because of it. One, I am very open-minded to their perception of events that they have witnessed. Two, I also understand that it is their perception. This awareness helps us to investigate sans bias; we can let the location speak for itself and our equipment capture that conversation. Sometimes, we have our own personal experiences while at these locations, but that simply fuels the conversation between location and equipment. We will rush to an area with night vision cameras and EMF detectors, hoping to catch a glimpse of what could have caused the perceived personal experience. Often, the conversation is not captured—it remains a secret told to the perceiver, precious but ultimately frustrating.

In an article titled "Visual Perception Theory," Saul McLeod, a psychology tutor at the University of Manchester, wrote, "In order to receive information from the environment we are equipped with sense organs, e.g. eye, ear, nose. Each sense organ is part of a sensory system which receives sensory inputs and transmits sensory information to the brain. … A major theoretical issue on which psychologists are divided is the extent to which perception relies directly on the information present in the stimulus. Some argue that perceptual processes are not direct, but depend on the perceiver's expectations and previous knowledge as well as the information available in the stimulus itself."

Which is an excellent point; if previous knowledge and expectations make up a part, if not all, of a perceived version of events, how are we supposed to accurately investigate a potentially paranormal location based on that? What I have found is that it can be done simply by removing bias. Or it can be done based on equipment alone, or with a rational investigator who fully understands their surroundings and has a foundation of rational behavior and rational responses. When you combine readings from an EMF detector, the monitoring of temperature, and the scrutinizing of audio and video recordings with a professional, rational investigator, perception is no longer limited to an individual's viewpoint but morphs into something that is closer to fact, or to unbiased evidence that was captured perception-free.

So, what are we supposed to do with this perception-free evidence? Simply post it on a paranormal website or share it on YouTube or Facebook? How do we advance to doing scientifically defined and universally accepted paranormal research? If we find a way, we can extend it to UFO investigations as well. Ufology, in my opinion, falls under the paranormal phenomena umbrella, and techniques used in ghost-hunting can translate. I have tried this in my field work, using similar methods of evidence collection. This includes photo and video documentation, telepathy, and the interviewing of witnesses. I suppose we could submit our findings to scientific research institutes, but they are already burdened with real-world concerns. Or we could try to find an open-minded scientist, such as Michio Kaku, but then what? I do not have the answer. I only have what I would like to see, which is an open-minded scientific organization dedicated to studying the paranormal—a SETI Institute for all things paranormal, if you will. Guess what? There was one, called NIDSci (National Institute for Discovery Science), which was in operation between 1995 and 2004. Based in Las Vegas, Nevada, and privately financed, it was the brainchild of real-estate developer Robert Bigelow, whose goal was to research and support studies in the paranormal and fringe sciences, especially ufology.

Could an organization like NIDSci exist again, and what sort of funding would it need? Could we do even better than NIDSci, creating an organization that is run and paid for by forward-thinking scientists and activists instead of an eccentric billionaire (who rarely shared results)? There are many ways that funding could happen. Currently, funding for the SETI Institute is provided by a multitude of sources. There is no government funding for SETI; however, there are other astrobiology research projects happening at SETI that are sometimes funded by NASA and the National Science Foundation.

Regardless, how does that help anyone now? Just by discussing the topic, though, I feel we are headed toward a better place. Imagine if ridicule was eliminated, bias gone, and instead we were open-minded to any claim or every claim of the paranormal. This may sound ludicrous, but stop and think about the implications for a moment. For example, I personally do not believe in the Loch Ness Monster or psychics (I believe Loch Ness to be an eel, and while some psychics are extremely accurate and I enjoy the work of Chip Coffey, a believer is not what I would call myself). With that said, I *am* a believer in Bigfoot, extraterrestrials, and crop circles. And despite my individual beliefs, I would most certainly entertain evaluating Loch Ness Monster evidence and psychic claims. Couple this open-mindedness with a scientific approach, and numerous areas of opportunity open for us. When bias is removed, so is judgment. When judgment is removed, we get more people submitting reports. And when we get more reports, the sample size grows exponentially, painting a rather large and complex paranormal algorithm.

Peter Davenport, founder of the National UFO Reporting Center (NUFORC), and Leland Bechtel, former MUFON State Director for Maine, have both said that nearly 90 percent of UFO encounters from around the world go unreported. This may be due in part to simply not knowing how to report a sighting, but fear of ridicule can play a large role as well. In a conversation that I had with NUFORC in March of 2014, we agreed that if witnesses could get past these obstacles, having a larger sample size of reports would only help further the research of the UFO phenomenon.

Understanding why this is important is a great first step. In my opinion, it is important to get as much data as possible, despite the presence or absence of belief. The raw data always gets processed, and what we are left with is much like that conversation between location and equipment that I described earlier (hint: *perception-free evidence*).

An example of how this process is in fact already occurring can be found in an apparent UFO sighting that took place at Acadia National Park in September of 2009. The Acadia Night Sky Festival sponsored a nighttime photography workshop, led by an astronomer, in the park. At around 8:00 p.m. EST, the workshop participants had set up their cameras near Eagle Lake, pointing toward the southwest, when a bright object appeared in the sky. On the website *Phantoms & Monsters,* one participant describes it as follows: "It seemed to come down in the sky, burn brightly, creating a cone of light shining toward the ground much like a streetlight, and fog-like light around it ... " It was observed for a few moments and then disappeared. Fortunately, the participants photographed the event. You can see the photo with a quick Google Image search for "Acadia UFO."

MUFON received numerous reports about this "cone of light" from various areas in New England, the Eastern United States, and Canada, including Connecticut, Maryland, New York, New Jersey, Pennsylvania, West Virginia, Nova Scotia, and Maine. However, despite the strangeness of the event—even for those who spend a good deal of time studying the sky—it turns out there was a practical explanation. In response to many concerned calls to local news stations, CNN reported that the cone of light was caused by an experimental rocket launch from NASA's Wallops Flight Facility in Virginia. The agency explained that the light "came from an artificial noctilucent cloud formed by the exhaust particles" as the rocket entered the upper atmosphere. NASA said that "observation stations on the ground and in satellites will track the artificial noctilucent clouds created by the rocket for months" and that "data collected during the experiment will provide insight into the formation, evolution, and properties of noctilucent clouds, which are typically observed naturally at high latitudes."

Oh perception, how vulnerable you can make us. How lovely your experiences can be. Also, what a great data point for the continuing conversation between equipment, location, and perceiver! A sighting occurred, pictures were taken, perceptions abounded, and an explanation was found. The perception of many of the witnesses followed an organic path to factual reality, not to a perceived reality. Overall, then, while the phenomenon was identified as not a UFO, the open-minded skepticism that occurred is a good lesson in how paranormal inquiries can be of valid concern and conducted for valid reasons.

Keep this thought in mind while reading the rest of this book. Some of the witness claims in the stories reported may seem fantastic and downright unbelievable, but always remember—it's someone's unique perception.

2

NINETEENTH-CENTURY UFOS

Merriam-Webster's definition of folklore is "*1*: traditional customs, tales, sayings, dances, or art forms preserved among a people; *2*: a branch of knowledge that deals with folklore; *3*: an often-unsupported notion, story, or saying that is widely circulated." It is possible that quite some time from now this entire book could be considered folklore. One thing that folklore has bred, besides the stories themselves, is "folk-belief." In his foreword to the book *Wonders in the Sky: Unexplained Aerial Objects from Antiquity to Modern Times*, Dr. David J. Hufford writes that "this term was, and still is, generally reserved for beliefs that are at odds in some way with the official modern worldview." This sounds a lot like it could be describing ufology.

Medieval and other early civilizations have described UFOs as "flying shields" and contemplated the idea of humans from the sky, or what we now call "star people." A famous sighting of unexplained flying objects was depicted in a 1561 Nuremberg woodcut, where the "globes" and a "spear" were shown in the midst of an aerial fight with one another before descending in smoke to the earth. (Search "Nuremberg woodcut" on the web to see this fascinating image.) Also, there are numerous stories from the New England area, including one from 1644 in Boston, Massachusetts, where witnesses observed "man-shaped lights"; one from the Bay of Fundy in 1796 where fifteen "ships" were seen flying in the air; and an 1820 story from New Hampshire where a man claimed to have been followed home by "several glowing balls."

The state of Maine had UFO and extraterrestrial folklore of its own just waiting to be uncovered. Two stories from the early nineteenth century are recounted below. The sightings they depict remain unexplained to this day.

Abraham's Encounter

The first paranormal investigator in the United States could very well be Reverend Abraham Cummings. He was a skeptic with an inquisitive mind. He was well educated, having received a master's degree from Brown University. In 1826, he first published his book entitled *Immortality Proved by the Testimony of Sense: In Which is Contemplated the Doctrine of Spectres and the Existence of a Particular Spectre Addressed to the Candor of this Enlightened Age.* It tells the tale of Nelly Butler, a poor young woman who tragically passed away in the small town of Sullivan, Maine, but continued to be seen by hundreds of townspeople for years after her death. Starting in 1799, Nelly communicated, it was said, with multiple groups of people at the same time, almost begging for belief in her afterlife. Abraham Cummings shared reports that "she promised nearly fifty people to convince them of her being such as she professed to be … " He spoke with numerous eye witnesses during his investigation, some of whom said they would see Nelly in "personal form" roaming the fields, roads, and pathways. Others reported hearing her disembodied voice, or witnessing "a mere mass of light."

Five years later, Rev. Cummings had an encounter one evening with an entity in a field. He presented a firsthand account of this "spectre in the field." I ask you to challenge yourself while you read the following tale: Does the event he describes read more like a ghost story, or more like an encounter with an extraterrestrial being?

On a mild July evening in Maine, the reverend was sought out by two men. They had just been crossing the field near town when they saw what they believed was the spectre; in earlier sightings, this being was described as being "white as the light" and moving "like a cloud above the ground in personal form and magnitude." After their encounter, they were naturally distressed and eager to share their story with Cummings. The reverend was certainly intrigued by their claims and assured them that he would investigate.

I can picture him as he walked toward the field, the sun setting. He was curious to discover what had frightened the men so badly, so he purposefully looked for anything out of place. He eventually observed a white rock a distance away on the ground, which did not at first seem unusual. But then, without warning, the "rock" began to ascend. Cummings watched in amazement, for it appears to have been glowing brightly. He had been sure that the two men he'd spoken to earlier were drunk, mistaken, or both, but here he was, alone and witness to the very thing they'd told him about. He described the event in detail: "The white rock was in the air; its form a complete Globe, white with a tincture of red, like the damask rose, and its diameter about two feet." As he gazed upon the spectacle, it suddenly came toward him, and he saw something emerge from the white globe. He gawked at its oddness and described it as "a personal form with a female dress, but [it] did not appear taller than a girl seven years old."

It is interesting to note that the entity Rev. Cummings saw was depicted as small and child-sized. The stereotypical "alien" is often described in this manner. It is also worth noting that he appears to have spoken telepathically with the being as it stood before him. Although he was convinced that this entity was the ghost of Nelly Butler, it looked nothing like her description. He was confused by this and wanted to communicate with it but found that he could not speak, so instead he thought of what he wanted to say. He recounted that "while I looked upon her, I said in my mind, 'you are not tall enough for the woman who has so frequently appeared among us.' Immediately she grew up as large and as tall as I considered that woman to be."

Perhaps this is more conjecture on my part, but Cummings seemed to describe the being as shape-shifting right in front of him, taking the form of a recognizable figure, as in the movie *Contact.* Toward the end of that movie, Jodie Foster's character has a scene with an alien that shows itself in the form of someone familiar to her. Maybe this was what happened in Cummings's case. Then again, perhaps he was speaking in some sort of hyperbolic sense. Or maybe he could not find the words to accurately describe his encounter. Furthermore, maybe the figure did not appear as a woman at all and "spectre" was his only and closest word for it. Because of that, he may have formed the opinion that the entity had a femininity to it. The following statement might support this idea: "On her head was the representation of the sun diffusing the luminous, rectilinear rays every way to the ground." This is more conjecture, and I don't mean to go all *Ancient Aliens* on you, but this certainly sounds more like Egyptian descriptions of gods such as the Kachinas or the Anunnaki and less like a ghost.

Moments after the encounter, it seems, Cummings was suddenly inside his home without quite knowing how he got there. At this point, both the entity and the "rock" were gone.

Abductions and encounters with extraterrestrials are often associated with missing time and confusion as to how one arrived at a different location. You can refer to the Travis Walton case, the Betty and Barney Hill abductions, and the stories "The Woman Who Time Forgot" and "The Great Escape!," found later in this book, for examples of this.

Reverend Abraham Cummings continued writing books and conducting investigations of the unknown after this encounter, though none come across quite as otherworldly as this one.

The Educator and the Light

In 1978, the *Courier-Freeman* newspaper (Potsdam, NY) published an article titled "Diary Describes UFO Seen In 1808." In it, a woman named Cynthia Everett is described as having had a peculiar sighting one evening in Camden, Maine. The event, like Cummings's incident, occurred in the month of July, and Everett wrote of her experience in a diary. Interestingly, the discovery of this encounter was happenstance. In 1978, Dr. Judith Becker Ranlett, a historian and professor for State University College at Potsdam, was conducting research for a Women's History project she was working on. The research included a diary loaned to her by her father-in-law; Cynthia Everett was Dr. Ranlett's husband's great-great-grandmother.

An educated woman and teacher, Everett began keeping the diary in 1804 and wrote about her life, daily events, and observations. Dr. Ranlett felt as though she truly came to understand who Cynthia Everett was through reading the massive 600-page diary. She observed that Everett was not prone to fantasies of any kind.

Everett would typically write in her diary just before retiring for the evening, and the night of her encounter was no different. A light outside caught her eye. I can imagine her seated on her bed, having just finished her evening ablutions, when she saw it through the window, then rising quickly and fumbling for her diary. She wrote, "At the first sight, I thought it was a Metier, but from its motion I soon perceived it was not." The diary entry continues with "it seemed to dart at first as quickly as light; and appeared to be in the Atmosphere, but lowered toward the ground and kept on at an equal distance sometimes ascending and sometimes descending. It moved round in the then visable Horison (it was not very light) and then returned back again…"

That is where her encounter ends, and she did not write of any other sightings.

Given that Everett was educated in astronomy, Ranlett found it interesting that she did not speculate about other natural possibilities for what the light could have been other than a meteor, which she'd quickly dismissed. Everett had written about earthquakes and the appearance of a comet prior to this entry. Ranlett said, "She was the kind of person who would have explained it as a natural phenomenon, if she could have." Everett was twenty-four years old at the time of this odd diary entry, and she stopped writing in it once she was married.

What do you think the light could have been? In 1808, few man-made lights were in the sky. Some of the few that existed at the time were Chinese lanterns and hot-air balloons. Perhaps it could have been one of these, though one would think that a hot-air balloon would not have been mistaken for a meteor, as Everett first described it. Yet whether extraterrestrial in nature or not, Everett saw something that evening that was significant enough for her to write about. I, for one, am thankful that she and Rev. Cummings had stories to add to Maine's extraterrestrial folklore.

THE GIRL WHO SAW MONSTERS

Settled in 1774 and once called Taylor Town, Union, Maine, is located in the Mid-Coast region of the state. Union is home to the Maine Blueberry Festival, the Maine Antique Festival and, of course, the Union Fair. As you drive through George's River Scenic Byway on Route 235, you'll find a unique mixture of beautiful shores on one side of the road and thick forests on the other. If you were to delve a little deeper, into the residents of this historic town, you would discover a hardworking, agriculturist community that painstakingly runs dairy farms, blueberry fields, wineries, and an assortment of service-related businesses. The people of Union certainly have a knack for harnessing and harvesting the earth beneath their feet, but has anyone thought about the sky above? Is an unintentional blind eye turned?

One woman knows the horror of looking up. This is her story.

I first heard of Laura Dent (pseudonym) from MUFON'S television program *Hangar 1: The UFO Files*. As I watched the episode, I was angry at myself for not knowing about the story sooner. A quick search of the MUFON database provided Dent's story in full, and it was also how I came to befriend MUFON's State Director for Maine, Valerie Schultz. I first contacted Schultz in May of 2016 to inquire about the case, and she explained, "I was the investigator. I remember it vividly. It was a case that had everything in it: crop circles, men in black who took samples of the grass and earth, a hovering disc-shaped craft, entities which were gray, and abductions!" I shared her enthusiasm about the elements of the case and we discussed Dent's incredible story at length. After you read the following tale, I ask you—and manage your thoughts carefully—is perception a reality in this case?

In 1981, while most Americans were swept up in the assassination attempt of Pope John Paul II and Ronald Reagan officially taking office, one little girl, aged eight, began looking toward the sky. She was not lying on her lawn in the carefree days of summer identifying animal shapes in the clouds. Instead, this poor girl was trying her very best to sleep in her bed when lights from "somewhere above" engulfed her family's farm. On one particular night, she awoke to a bright light illuminating her bedroom. Cautiously, she approached her window, and the light faded.

The next morning, she went downstairs to talk about the previous night's bright lights. Her parents seemed dismissive and figured she had been dreaming. Night fell and the little girl drifted off to sleep. Hours passed and then the illumination started again; her eyes stirred under closed lids. The intensity of the light grew and her eyes popped open. She stood, awestruck, and walked to the window; the light was low over the field this time. Frighteningly low. She squinted and could make out an object that was stationary in the field, though it was too far away for her to identify any sort of shape. A tractor, maybe, but the timing seemed too out of place based on what she knew about her father's farming. She really wanted to go out into the field to see where the light could be coming from, but fear held her back. She decided once again to wait until morning. This time she would be insistent with her father so he would really hear what she had to say. When she awoke the next morning, she found her parents had already left for town to run a couple of errands. She decided, with renewed bravado in the daylight, to go to the field by herself to see if there were signs of anything having been there. As she approached the area thought to be where the light had come from, she started to get an odd feeling. She then realized that she had stepped into an unusual, out-of-place opening in the field. The girl looked all around, startled because she was standing in a circular-shaped bed of neatly laid grass. None of this seemed right to her, and she slowly stepped out of the circle and ran back up to the house.

When her parents arrived home, she told them about the light from the previous evening and about the odd circle that she had just found in the field. Her father was concerned, and rightly so due to the potential damage to his hay crop. They went down to the field so his daughter could show him what she had found. When they stepped into the circle, her father was visibly confused. He looked all around in shock. As they investigated the field, they found more areas of neatly laid grass. Some were little rectangle shapes connecting to other, smaller circles and then back to the original, larger circle. Her father ran back to the farmhouse and climbed onto the roof for a better look, and was astonished to see a full-fledged crop circle in his field. His daughter asked him what he thought it could be. He responded by saying it was just someone playing a prank on him again. He said this with anxious eyes that the little girl noticed and thought, *Again?* Her father mowed the field that same day, removing any evidence of the crop circle having been there.

A few days later, the girl's folks went to town and again she stayed behind. Not ten minutes had passed when an unknown vehicle came driving up to the house. The girl saw the vehicle approach, became frightened, and hid underneath a pear tree that was surrounded by some old farm equipment. As the car pulled to a stop, the girl peeked out and got a very good look at the car and its occupants. She explained, "This car was black. Black wheels, black windows, black everything and no plate. The people were also dressed in black." Two men got out of the car and started walking to the freshly mowed field, right toward where the crop circle had been just a few days prior. It astonished the girl that they knew the exact spot of where the anomaly had been, especially since the area had become indiscernible after her father had mowed. She observed the men taking soil and grass samples and placing them inside small jars. Once finished, they returned to their vehicle and left.

This experience frightened yet fascinated her, and she opted to keep it to herself. Every night after that she would stay up, waiting for the light to show itself. She did not have to wait long. A few nights later, the white light slowly started illuminating her room. She jumped out of bed, grabbed her binoculars, and began watching. The light faded and she observed a silver, disc-shaped craft with windows in the field. Surrounding the border of the craft were a series of multicolored lights—red, white, green, blue, and orange. She watched in amazement as the object appeared to hover mere feet above the field. What she saw next would change her life forever.

As she watched the craft, she noticed some shadows that moved around the field. She thought they might be animals and kept watching. Finally, the shadows came into focus. This little girl, with a mind that was still developing, was now faced with interpreting what she saw next. Binoculars at her eyes, she observed humanoid figures in the field. She felt relatively safe in the confines of her room and stared in wonder. She described the figures as small, slender, and gray in color, with bulging heads and black eyes. She thought of all the sci-fi movies she had seen throughout the years and whispered to herself, "They're real."

Fast-forward a couple of years and hundreds of sightings later. The girl woke up to find that a strange mark had appeared on her right hand. She described it as "between my pointing and middle finger in the shape of a triangle. It hasn't always been there." At one point, she touched the mark, became light-headed, and fainted. She said that while she was in this state, someone or something telepathically spoke to her and explained that the mark should not be removed. It warned that if she did remove it, she would find another mark someplace else. It was at this point that she finally understood that she had been abducted.

Now an adult, she still has trouble remembering most aspects of her abductions. She remembered her abductors being nice and playful with her when she was younger. But as she got older, she felt they became less accommodating and more devious in nature.

For most people, encounters of "the fourth kind"—alien abduction—can be a far-fetched concept to think about. Those who experience it claim that extraterrestrial creatures are kidnapping individuals around the world.

Experiencers will come back with accounts of a multitude of procedures that seem to be medical in nature. According to writer Eugene Braxton, many abductees describe their encounters as "terrifying or humiliating, but others describe them as transformative or even pleasant."

In the book *UFO Abductions: The Measure of a Mystery,* researcher Thomas Bullard presented an "abduction narrative" that describes the general sequence of events. Its condensed form is as follows:

- Capture: The abductee is somehow rendered incapable of resisting and is taken from terrestrial surroundings to an apparent alien spacecraft.

- Examination and Procedures: Invasive physiological and psychological procedures, and on occasion simulated behavioral situations, training and testing, or sexual liaisons.

- Loss of Time: Abductees often rapidly forget the majority of their experience, either as a result of fear, medical intervention, or both.

- Return: The abductees are returned to Earth, occasionally in a different location from where they were allegedly taken or with new injuries or disheveled clothing.

- Aftermath: The abductee must cope with the psychological, physical, and social effects of the experience.

In the case of Laura Dent from Union, regardless of your opinion on alien abductions, perception is reality—and she described a reality that is most certainly otherworldly.

A CURIOUS OCCURRENCE IN ANSON

In an approximately one hundred square mile area of Somerset and Franklin counties, Maine, traveling west to east, you will find the towns of Farmington, Industry, New Sharon, Starks, Anson, Madison, Norridgewock, and Skowhegan, among others. You can get to these towns via Route 43 or an offshoot of it, which crosses the beautiful Kennebec River. Even if you have traveled this route before, or some of its offshoots (Routes 148, 2, etc.), you may not have known of the numerous reports of UFO activity in the area. These reports range from inconspicuous Close Encounters of the First Kind all the way to the complex Close Encounters of the Fourth Kind (definitions for all Close Encounter classifications are provided at the end of this chapter). The witnesses who gave these reports range from retired Naval officers and sheriffs to local townspeople.

Between 1981 and 2009, the area that I have dubbed "the Somerset Triangle" has boasted over two hundred sightings, as reported by NUFORC, MUFON, the Somerset County Sheriff's Department, the *Portland Press Herald*, the *Morning Sentinel*, and the *Sun Journal*. As discussed in the chapter "Only a Step Away," if we are to also include an estimate of the sightings that go unreported, we may be looking at upward of eight hundred to one thousand encounters in just this area alone! I wrote about the towns in the Somerset Triangle in my first book, interesting stories from Starks and Industry that I suggest you read for yourself. Another noteworthy encounter, this one from Anson, I have included here. It occurred in 2007 at the home of Gheri Rinaldi and her family. I spoke with Gheri in June of 2016; this is her story.

The Valentine's Day Blizzard of 2007 was in full swing in the Midwestern United States. This storm also affected the northeast, which caused an inordinate amount of ice to fall throughout New England. The town of Anson avoided the bulk of the storm, though fresh snow had fallen. But snow and ice were the last things on Gheri's mind, since she was enjoying celebrating her son's fourteenth birthday. After cake, Gheri went out on her deck for a cigarette when a light behind some trees caught her attention. She watched this light for a moment as it moved sideways through the woods. Confused by what the source of the light could be, she called out for her son to join her outside. "Honey, look over there," she said as he walked outside. "What *is* that?!" She pointed to the area by the trees. He saw the light but had no explanation to offer his mother. After a few moments, the movement of the light became erratic, and though their view was obstructed by trees, they estimated that the light was about one hundred to one hundred fifty feet in the sky. They described the color as orange-yellow, with what appeared to be an aura-type glow around it.

The boy turned to his mother and noticed she still had the camera around her neck from taking pictures during the party. "Mom, take a picture!" he said. Gheri looked down excitedly at the camera and proceeded to raise it toward the sky. She focused in on the light and ... nothing. The camera would not work. She tried again but the device failed. Frustrated, and assuming her camera had dead batteries, she went inside the house to exchange them for fresh ones. As soon as she entered her home, the camera went off! "Wow, I must have done something wrong," she thought and went back outside. She raised her camera once more, but it still would not work. Both she and her son went inside this time and he went to fetch some new batteries. Once installed, he took a test picture; it worked just fine, so the boy took the camera back outside, hoping the odd light was still there. Gheri followed behind and was shocked to see that there were now four lights hovering behind the trees. Her son yelled, "Mom, there's more of them!" He quickly raised the camera for a shot, but again it would not function, so they gave up on the camera.

Out of nowhere, the four lights shot out of the trees and into plain view, maintaining their altitude of approximately one hundred fifty feet. The four lights then went vertical, one on top of the other, and shot back into the trees. This is a similar description to the Stephenville lights that occurred in Texas in 2008 (a year after this sighting), which had numerous eyewitnesses who saw vertical lights. (A great telling of that story, including a reenactment of the lights, was made courtesy of the *Alien Mysteries* television program and can be viewed in full on YouTube.)

The pair could only watch in amazement, but it was just too weird for them, so Gheri told her son, "Go grab my phone, I'm calling 911, this is crazy." The operator at the Somerset County Communications Center could hear the excitement and fear in her voice. "There's something in the sky right now," Gheri said. "Do you have any idea what it might be? Are there any military maneuvers happening?" The operator said they had fielded multiple calls about the lights from towns in the surrounding area. "So I'm not crazy?" Gheri said with relief in her voice. The operator told Gheri that she was not and that a Deputy Sheriff was on his way to the location.

The *Morning Sentinel* newspaper reported, in the article "They Saw Strange Lights in the Sky," that Deputy Richie Putnam, who did not see the lights himself, did put a call in to the Federal Aviation Administration and the Brunswick Naval Air Station, which both stated that they did not have any flights in the area. Putnam did discover that the Vermont Air National Guard had conducted practice maneuvers that night in the vicinity. Marie Endsley, spokeswoman for the Guard, said in response to the *Morning Sentinel's* inquiry, "We were conducting our normal training missions and were flying through there." She did not confirm the towns or county where the maneuvers took place.

In my opinion, it seems odd that the FAA would not be informed of practice maneuvers by the Vermont Air National Guard. When speaking with me, Gheri was convinced that it was not jets that she had seen, and added, "They were silent, often just hovering, and lasted for about an hour. Jets and flares cannot do that." In August of 2016, I called the Sheriff's Department multiple times about this 2007 incident. Messages left for Deputy Putnam were not returned.

About a week prior to Gheri's sighting, UFOs had been reported in the Farmington area, though described differently than the lights Gheri observed. Farmington is approximately fifteen miles from Anson and just about five miles south of Industry. Some witnesses to the Farmington sightings did comment that the lights were most likely flares from the often-seen military planes doing night maneuvers. Other witnesses said that while the color was similar to flares, their movements and duration of appearance were not like flares at all. According to the *Sentinel*, Marie

Endsley informed them that F-16s "fly lower than seven thousand feet" and "flares might look reddish-orange, but would disintegrate well before hitting the ground."

Somerset County Sheriff Barry A. DeLong, now retired, was involved with the investigation of the Anson sighting and takes the UFO phenomenon seriously due to having his own encounter thirty years prior. He explained to the *Sentinel* that the lights he saw in the 1970s "were hovering about 15 feet from my cruiser, late at night. . . . It had fixed lights that were spinning. It was huge, and oval-shaped. I knew it wasn't a jet fighter. It slowly started backing off toward Sugarloaf, and then at a terrific speed." While it is certainly possible that some branch of the military could have conducted practice missions, it most certainly *cannot* explain the multiple eye-witness accounts in which lights in the sky were observed hovering, and being maneuvered intelligently, for over an hour.

Ultimately, the explanation for the lights Gheri saw over Anson that evening was the National Guard's practice maneuvers. Gheri wholeheartedly disagrees. My lasting impression from my discussion with Gheri is that she is a genuine person who never thought twice about UFOs before this event. She has a captivating personality that reinforces her believability. And I believe her story.

Before ending our interview, I asked her if she'd had any other encounters since. "No, but my eyes are always to the sky now!" Same here, Gheri. Same here.

How Close Encounters Are Defined

As scientific advisor to the United States Air Force from 1947 to 1969, J. Allen Hynek conducted UFO studies for them through Project Sign, Project Grudge, and Project Blue Book. He created the original classification system for UFO and alien encounters, which he published in his first book, *The UFO Experience: A Scientific Inquiry.* His colleague Jacques Vallee established the CE-4 classification in his *Journal of Scientific Exploration* article entitled "Five Arguments Against the Extraterrestrial Origin of Unidentified Flying Objects." A basic overview of the categories is as follows:

- Close Encounter of the First Kind (CE-1):
  A sighting of one or more unidentified
  flying objects.

- Close Encounter of the Second Kind (CE-2):
  Observing a UFO, and associated physical
  effects from the UFO.

- Close Encounter of the Third Kind (CE-3):
  Observing "animate beings" in association
  with a UFO sighting.

- Close Encounter of the Fourth Kind (CE-4):
  Alien abduction, or direct communication
  with an animate being.

- Nocturnal Lights: Unexplainable light sources at night.

- Daylight Discs: Generally oval or disc-shaped, metallic in appearance, sighted during the daytime.

- Radar/Visual: Unidentified "blips" on radar screens that coincide with and confirm simultaneous visual sightings.

Dr. Steven Greer (The CE-5 Initiative), Michael Naisbitt (CE-6), and the Black Vault website (CE-7) have offered additional, lesser known classifications.

- Close Encounters of the Fifth Kind (CE-5): Bilateral contact experiences through conscious, voluntary, and proactive human-initiated communication with extraterrestrials.

- Close Encounters of the Sixth Kind (CE-6): Death of a human or animal associated with a UFO sighting.

- Close Encounters of the Seventh Kind (CE-7): The creation of a human/alien hybrid, either by sexual reproduction or by artificial scientific methods.

5

VILLAGE OF THE STRANGE

A bright light, oddly out of place, was seen behind some trees in the backyard of a young man from southern Maine. The lights descended and gradually faded. As the witness lowered his hand, having no need to shield his eyes, he saw that a disc-shaped craft had landed in his backyard. He said that the door to the craft was open, and he watched as a ramp was lowered.

No, I did not just provide the logline for *E.T., part 2.* Instead, what I provided is the beginning of a Close Encounter of the Fourth Kind from the town of Eliot. (See what I did there? Eliot, E.T. . . . never mind.) The small town is a family-oriented community, situated just across the river from Portsmouth, New Hampshire.

The town of Eliot was once known as the Middle Parish of the town of Kittery, eventually establishing itself as its own town in 1810. Fast-forward about 160 years and you will find that there were reports of strange encounters in the sky. Below are a few of those reports.

The UFO Flap of '66

In the book *Creatures of the Outer Edge*, Jerome Clark and Loren Coleman write about a letter they received from Betty Hill (yes, the Betty Hill of abduction fame) about an encounter that a group of New Hampshire UFO researchers had during a visit to Eliot. Betty explained that fleets of UFOs would "fly up" the Piscataqua River almost every evening in the spring of 1966. It became so persistent that people from all over southern Maine and New Hampshire would drive to Eliot to watch the UFOs, and the police were even called in to manage congestion that all the traffic caused. Betty went on to write that it was such a spectacular event, with so many people, that food carts had set up along the road and people brought telescopes and binoculars to catch a glimpse.

On the evening the UFO research group arrived, they drove around the area to look for a spot to set up their equipment. They eventually found a gravel pit that provided a small amount of privacy so they could conduct their observations. Betty explained what happened next: "A huge, dark 'dog' ran through the pit. The dog was larger than any they knew so they decided to try to follow it. They ran through the pit, but the last one in line was stopped by a strange odor. He could not identify it, and as he stood there, a large form glided towards him. The form was giving off this odor, and he had the feeling he was to follow this gliding form." At this point, the rest of the group had no idea what had happened to their missing colleague. After searching for the dog and the researcher, the rest of the team returned to where their cars were parked. When they arrived, the missing researcher unexpectedly appeared. He behaved aggressively and tried to run from the group. They watched in disbelief and struggled to restrain him. Once he was calm and more himself, the group decided that they'd had enough with the odd occurrences in Eliot and left the gravel pit.

Clark and Coleman also wrote in their book about the association of large black dog sightings and UFO activity, uncovering stories of black dog encounters along with UFO activity in Savannah, Georgia, and as far away as South Africa. For further research, I highly recommend the double edition publication of their books *The Unidentified & Creatures of the Outer Edge*, available from Anomalist Books.

In the book *UFOs: Interplanetary Visitors*, Raymond Fowler writes of another encounter from this 1966 flap, from a witness named Madeline Huntress. She was on Route 101 in Eliot when she saw a light above the power lines. The light dimmed as she approached, which revealed an oval-shaped object with a domed top. She estimated its diameter as sixteen to twenty-seven feet. She observed windows in the craft but was unable to see inside. Due to the frightened state that Mrs. Huntress was in, she sped off, with her entire sighting lasting approximately sixty seconds. She did report her encounter to authorities the next day.

In researching the follow-up to this story, I contacted the Eliot police department. They told me that their records do not go as far back as 1966, but that they would check. As of this writing, I have not heard back.

Remember the Ramp!

In the summer of 1977, a few days after July 4th, Daniel (pseudonym) woke up to a bright light that shined through his bedroom window. He shielded his eyes, squinted, and saw a light behind a row of trees in his backyard. Quickly, it moved higher into the air and then slowly descended into his backyard. Once landed, the light faded and a craft could be seen. Daniel saw that some sort of door had opened with a ramp extended out of it (input classic sci-fi movie imagery). He simply could not believe the sight that was before him. He tried to comprehend what happened, but the experience only got stranger when he heard a voice inside his head. In his account of the event on *UFO Evidence*, Daniel explained, "I could 'hear' a message in my thoughts that my desire for proof of extraterrestrials had arrived and that I was not to tell anyone. It was definitely telepathic communication..."

Confused and startled by the craft *and* the telepathic communication, he woke his girlfriend. He asked if she could see the craft as well. She saw it and shared that she had received a message transmitted inside her head, too. She said, "It's telling us not to tell anyone and that we can come onto the ship." Daniel was filled with excitement and quickly darted out of the bedroom, to the backyard. He stared at the craft for a moment, then ran up the ramp. He wrote that he could see inside the craft and described it as having "a yellowish light coming from the interior and I could see a tiled wall and what appeared to be a tube filled with liquid at the center of the room." And then, nothing! Daniel blacked out.

Moments later, he found himself back inside his house, only in his underwear, and felt as though he had been gone for quite a while. Did he think that they may have been abducted? He did not elaborate, but added that his girlfriend was in the room. Once he realized he was back inside his house, he immediately ran back outside. At this point, the UFO hovered above the backyard as before. Suddenly, the UFO transformed itself into a US military cargo plane and, "complete with a rumbling engine sound," it "proceeded to fly away above the trees."

Once the "plane" was out of sight, Daniel explained, he became doubtful about the experience and started to forget bits and pieces of what had transpired. It was like waking up from a dream, when the memory of it is just on the periphery of your mental consciousness, yearning to be remembered. At that moment, Daniel vowed that he would remember what he had seen and what he and his girlfriend had experienced together, and he wrote down every detail that he could remember. He knew the experience was real, but he just could not remember what had happened once he'd stepped inside that craft. One thing was for sure—he did remember running up that ramp.

Coffin in the Sky

The house sat empty, except for the small family that was spending their last night there before moving to Alaska. Relocating to a far-off location can be life-changing, but for one young man, who lay in a sleeping bag in a bare room, something else presented itself that evening that was just as impactful.

According to a story shared on *UFO Casebook*, the radio was playing as Tobias (pseudonym) thought about how different his life was going to be once he and his family were settled into their new Alaskan home. While he contemplated this, something outside his bedroom window caught his eye. He noticed an out-of-place object in the sky flying in an erratic manner. He described it as "a black, geometric object zigzagging rapidly in the air above the tree line of the woods behind my house. Its distance away from me was about one and a half football field lengths. Its motion reminded me of an air hockey puck, with seemingly instantaneous changes in direction."

Tobias quickly forgot about Alaska, that bare room, and the life changes ahead, and slowly got up and peered out the window for a better look. Mouth agape, he saw what he described as a coffin-shaped object that quietly hovered ten feet above the treetops. The object then dipped behind the trees and Tobias lost sight of it. He was poised at the window, wondering what the object could have been and where it had suddenly gone. He thought it might be a military maneuver, or maybe he hadn't seen anything at all. Perhaps he had fallen asleep and it was simply a dream. He lay back down and continued listening to the radio. But something hadn't felt right. He couldn't close his eyes as the wonder of the sighting kept him awake. His young mind raced in all directions.

He peered out the window again and low and behold, it was back! He immediately got up, eyes wide. The object, about the size of a car, hovered right in his backyard, at the same height as his window and only thirty to forty feet away! He gasped and stared intently, studying every inch of the object. He described the second encounter this way: "It looked like it was made of metal, but was a dull gun-metal black, with no windows, lights, doors, or seams of any kind, but it did have a few small protrusions which looked like instrumentation—giving me the impression the object was some sort of machinery." Because the object was so close, he saw that it was shaped more like a cone with a flat tip than a coffin. No sooner had he observed this than the object instantly ascended and was out of sight.

He was left at the window again, and knew this time that he had not dreamed the event. If it was military, in his opinion, it must certainly be considered top secret. The experience startled him, but it wasn't necessarily frightening. He racked his brain for a plausible explanation as he knelt at that window. He hoped the object would come back so he could study it more. He decided to lie back down. After a few minutes, he realized that the radio was still on and the announcer was discussing UFOs due to the show receiving calls about a UFO over Eliot. He called in to the show and told his story.

There were no other sightings for Tobias that evening, or even to this date, but the wonder of that encounter never left him. Now an adult and working as an engineer, he is more intrigued than ever about his encounter. He now has an educated understanding of aeronautical physics and described the flight characteristics of the UFO: "It didn't need to move to stay aloft. It seemed unaffected by gravity or inertia. It had the ability to change speed and direction instantaneously—including the ability to hover perfectly still."

Reports from Eliot are still coming in to this day. During my correspondence with the Eliot police department, they advised me that if I am in the area and see anything out of the ordinary, I should call their non-emergency number. You best bet that I will.

6

WHEN THE SKY ROARED

In 1649, a gentleman by the name of Christopher Lawson purchased land from the Abenaki tribe, though it would still be over a hundred years before the town of Richmond, Maine, would officially be established. In February of 1823, the town was finally incorporated and took its name from a fort that had been built in the area in 1719. While the town is known for its old shipbuilding foundations due to its close vicinity to the Kennebec River, the community was also known for the manufacturing of boat materials, cobbling, and more.

Something the town is not known for are the odd sounds emanating from its sky. The phenomenon has been heard around the world and is typically referred to as "Doomsday Trumpets." These sounds could be compared to the blare of a trumpet (hence the name) and have been reported for hundreds of years, but recently have become better known through social media. Reports have come in from places in Germany, Russia, Australia, Canada, and the United States. There are numerous videos that you can watch on YouTube highlighting these sounds. Here are a couple you can look for right now: "Strange sounds in Conklin, Alberta" and "Trumpets of the Apocalypse—Sounds coming from the sky."

What could these sounds be and where could they be coming from? Recently, NASA offered an explanation stating that the sounds are earthbound and occur naturally, although they are often inaudible to the human ear. "If humans had radio antennas instead of ears, we would hear a remarkable symphony of strange noises coming from our own planet.... Earth's natural radio emissions are real and, although we're mostly unaware of them, they are around us all the time." Sounds fair enough. However, ponder the following:

In March of 2013, Richmond resident Tom Patrick (pseudonym) heard sounds like the ones from the aforementioned videos. It happened late at night between three and four in the morning. I contacted Tom in September of 2016 to discuss what he had heard. "The first experience was the more stunning experience," Tom told me as he wrestled for a rational explanation. "I was woken up by a rumbling. I live on the outskirts of a town of about thirty-three hundred people. It was like the sky was roaring. I thought to myself, well, what the hell is that?!" At first he'd considered the highway approximately two miles away from his house, and Brunswick Naval Air Station where perhaps a fleet of planes or jets was flying in or out. He'd even thought of snowplows on the road in front of his home, but it hadn't snowed at all, which was easily confirmed by glancing outside.

"And I looked out the window, but I didn't see anything," Tom said. "I'm on the second floor of my house and it sounded like a rocket overhead. But it was a constant roar. It sounded different. If you hear a jet or a plane, it has a crescendo and then trails off. This was not the case, just a constant sound for about ten minutes."

Tom discussed the sounds with friends, but none had heard them. He called the Maine State Police to inquire about the sounds, and took to Facebook to see if anyone else had heard anything. "I posted about this event on Facebook in the hopes that someone else might have heard the noise." He got no response from his posting and further explained, "However, being winter and the houses being buttoned up, I suspect most people either didn't hear the roaring or thought it a jet plane. Please note: Interstate 295 is about two miles from my house. There are no airports or train tracks for some twenty miles away. It was *not* snow plows. I called the (non-emergency) phone number of the police department to inquire if they had received any unusual reports of strange noises from the sky. I was told no such reports were called in."

More recently, on the evening of Sunday, April 9, 2017, residents from the towns of Gardiner, West Gardiner, Winthrop, Farmingdale, Kennebec, Skowhegan, and Augusta experienced earthquake-like tremors and heard a loud boom at around 9:00 p.m. The *Bangor Daily News* reported, in an article titled "Mystery Boom Befuddles Maine Authorities," that "the sound, described by various people as similar to an earthquake, a plane breaking the sound barrier and an explosion, prompted dozens of calls to Kennebec County dispatchers and Maine State Police." The state police investigated the odd occurrence by contacting the FAA for "planes down" and the National Weather Service to inquire about earthquake activity but came up empty-handed. Maine State Police spokesman Steve McCausland told the *Bangor Daily News*, "There's no explanation as to what residents were calling about."

Is There a Connection?

The *Bangor Daily News* reported, in an article titled "More Witnesses Report Seeing Bright-Colored County Fireball," that on January 27, 1998, there were numerous reports of explosion-like sounds and multiple fireball sightings observed in the skies of St. Agatha, Millinocket, Houlton, and Oakland, Maine. Between 8:30 and 10:30 p.m., two witnesses from Oakland reportedly heard two very loud blasts that shook their home, while at precisely the same time a woman who was on Interstate 95 in Houlton observed a fireball in the sky. Some witnesses in Millinocket saw the fireballs as well and reported hearing explosive sounds emanating from them.

There is a Project Blue Book report from 1964 that documents a fireball encounter in Millinocket. The report states that the fireball was on the side of the road and observed for over five minutes. The witnesses then got out of their vehicle for a better look, but became frightened and returned to their car, only to find that it would not start. The report concludes that the encounter was with a meteor. But with the witnesses' explanation that it was on the side of the road and seen for over five minutes, this conclusion does not make sense.

So, what did Tom hear in the skies that night? Could fireball UFOs be to blame? Maybe, but he did not see any lights. Could it simply be a natural phenomenon, as NASA explains and perhaps the fireballs themselves suggest—i.e., meteorites? I'm not sure. But I do feel that the phenomenon demands more research. Look up these sounds on YouTube; some of the recordings are downright creepy, to the point where one could really get caught up in the thought of an impending apocalypse.

For Tom, the possibilities are endless. He feels it could be anything—including extraterrestrials, the impending apocalypse, natural objects, or who knows. I share the same sentiment as Tom, but it gives me a sense of hope. This is a peculiar thought, I know. However, if this world never ceases to amaze us in spite of all the violence and political nonsense going on today, then maybe it's not all bad—and maybe there's still something to believe in.

THE MAN WHO FELL TO EARTH

Centuries ago, humanity believed that the Earth was at the center of the universe. In fact, fourth-century BC mythos adhered to a flat Earth theory, wherein a central axis ("axis mundi") was believed to join the Earth with the heavens and other realms. Given this Earth-centered focus, it's not surprsing that the search for intelligent life beyond our world has long been rooted in skepticism. Skepticism has also long surrounded scientific inquiries into the origin of life, due to the complexity of atoms and elements; or, to put it more simply, it was easy to conclude that the difficulty of getting the ingredients of life just right meant that the creation of life had to have been a fluke.

Wide-ranging attempts at explanations of life and the universe persisted, however. One interesting theory was put forth by Austrian scientist Hans Horbiger in 1913. His "World Ice Theory" was based on the idea that ice is "the basic substance of all cosmic processes," as historian Christina Wessely explained in her article "Cosmic Ice Theory—Science, Fiction, and the Public, 1894–1945." Horbiger believed that ice formed everything from planets and moons to the ether. In an effort to validate his work with the academic community, he promoted it in popular culture. The masses took enthusiastically to his fantastical concept, which suggests they found the academic science of the day less than satisfying.

As of late, however, you'll find more and more reputable scientists who are open to the idea of life existing beyond our planet, even beyond our solar system. With new findings of hundreds of extrasolar planets, distinguished and credible scientists are now arguing that there could be billions of Earth-like planets potentially teeming with life. Even though the recipe may be complex, the possibility that there is other intelligent life in our universe has certainly taken a 180 degree turn from most early philosophies on the subject.

While it's complex, life is also precious, and Mainers live a hard life (we're not the only ones by any means). Raising a family in our economic climate, with the stressors bred from that, is tough to endure. Even our extreme weather is a constant reminder of how treasured life really is. Because of all this, we have evolved to live the highest quality of life, despite anyone's individual circumstance. By this I mean that we adapt well to anything life throws at us. Against this background, there are some tried and true facts that we do live by—one of them being the importance of good weather. There is one season that every man, woman, and child in Maine looks forward to; it's coveted, it's short-lived, and we call it summer. Of course, we love our fall and all that comes with it, especially the leaves multichromatically morphing our landscape. And we have learned to make winter as fun as possible, with many outdoor recreation options available. But we hold dear the few short months that we get for summer. Our coasts transform into beautiful oceanside retreats. Tourists from all over flock to our great state to visit the likes of Bar Harbor, Acadia National Park, Wells, Ogunquit, Old Orchard Beach, and a variety of other spots. The season is fleeting, so we make the most of every day given to us.

One such tourist and his wife paid a visit to Maine in the summer of 1989. Their plan was to enjoy a week away from work and the bustling life of Massachusetts. One day during their stay in the Ogunquit area, the couple was walking along a shore path. Suddenly, the man became dizzy and confused, and had to clutch his wife's hand tightly to keep balance. His name was Ed, and he experienced an otherworldly encounter that changed his life forever.

John E. Mack, MD, a psychiatrist, hypnotist, professor at Harvard Medical School, and writer, conducted a study of two hundred men and women who claimed to have had alien abduction experiences. At the start of his study, he speculated that the majority if not all of the people he would be working with most likely suffered from some sort of mental illness. Once his work began, however, he found no signs of cognitive disabilities and began taking the alien abduction theory seriously. Ed, the tourist mentioned above, was one of Mack's case studies. In his book *Abduction: Human Encounters with Aliens,* Mack laid out the entire encounter and Ed's psychiatric visits with him.

On that shore path, Ed's anxious feeling eventually subsided, but the couple was concerned about what happened, so Ed sought medical attention. His doctor told him that he had high blood pressure and seemed overly stressed. Ed was working as a technician at a Massachusetts company; he enjoyed the work and thought stress from his job was not related to his malady. Suspecting a misdiagnosis from his doctor, he opted to try meditation and hoped it would alleviate the condition. Not long after this, he found himself remembering frightening images from his teenage years. The images confused him, and he tried to put the pieces together but it was all too strange. He did have a sense that the images were otherworldly in nature, and in 1992 he attended a conference of the Mutual UFO Network in New Hampshire. He talked with some of the attendees, who recommended that he reach out to psychiatrist John E. Mack. On July 23, 1992, Ed met with Mack, which initiated a four-month hypnosis regression period during which they uncovered a most unusual encounter.

The story for Ed started in the summer of 1961, when he was invited on a weeklong vacation with his friend's family to the coast of Maine. The family had rented a cabin on the beach for a week of fun, relaxation, and one last hoorah before the school year started up again. On one particularly warm evening, the two boys desperately wanted to sleep outside. They figured they could have a bit of fun without the watchful eyes of the parents. The mother was not thrilled at the idea of them sleeping on the beach by themselves, so she agreed that they could sleep in the family's vehicle with the windows down; the boys were ecstatic. As they settled in for their unsupervised sleepover, they discussed girls from their school, and as is common in early adolescent conversations, they discussed the topic of sex and which girls in their school they found most attractive. They giggled and laughed and thoroughly enjoyed their time in the car. The boys eventually drifted off to sleep, but Ed's slumber would not last long.

He was startled awake as he felt the car rock back and forth. He raised the back of his seat slightly so he could look out the window, and he heard someone walking around the car but saw nothing. He quickly lowered the seat, frightened that someone was lurking outside of the vehicle. He felt a buzzing sensation at the base of his neck and desperately tried to wake his friend, but the other boy was unresponsive. Ever so slightly, Ed raised his head and looked out the window again, recoiling in horror when he saw two big black eyes staring back at him. The buzzing sensation spread throughout his entire body, and he was slowly lifted from his seat by invisible forces and floated out of the window. Ed looked down and could see tiny figures with bulbous heads. He continued to float up into the air and out over the ocean. He heard the wind rushing by and saw the waves crashing against the rocks below. He was so scared at the thought of falling into the dark, watery abyss that he almost lost consciousness.

Just after he had that thought, a figure appeared before him and he could see that he was now in a room with transparent walls, but still above the ocean. Ed then observed that he was naked and the figure before him was female. He found her "attractively unusual" and felt self-conscious that he was not wearing clothes. The being spoke to him telepathically, saying, "You're okay. Don't fight it. Don't fight it." His fear diminished slightly and he looked around the odd room, which seemed to have changed again. It was some sort of amphitheater and there were more than a dozen other beings in the room with him; the female being sat across from him. He tried to speak to her but found that he could not talk. He then tried speaking telepathically to her and said, "How do you know me?" She looked at him kindly and thought, "I know what happened to you when you were younger. These things will not happen again." This confused Ed, but suddenly a bombardment of memories flooded into his head. He could only stare at her, with a newfound knowledge of his previous nightmarish alien abductions. He thought to the being, "Somehow or other you're doing a great job of convincing me that you're here for my well-being. I'm not just your laboratory rat, guinea pig." She assured him again that this time would be different, and that he would be okay. He believed her and his fear subsided completely.

Without warning, Ed suddenly experienced blood rush to his groin area. It felt out of place and almost forced. As he explained to Mack, "she's filling my mind with all sorts of erotic escapades ... She's just raising, somehow or other, she's just giving me, giving me a hard-on." Ed sat there and stared at the being, and again became self-conscious, especially with the other beings in the room. She looked at him as well, which gained his focus back onto her. He then had sexual thoughts about her and felt he could feel her inside of his head. She thought to him, "Yeah, you'd like that, wouldn't you, but that's not the way it's going to be." She then explained that her species needed human sperm to create "special babies." She said that this type of harvesting is to help the people of Earth. Again, he believed her and felt easily persuaded to help in what he called "their experiment." Ed's penis was then placed into a device that relaxed him. He explained, "It's a very smooth, hand-like thing. I want to believe it's her hand." He then ejaculated into the contraption. He looked at her, surprised at what happened, and she said they were pleased and had "gotten a good sample" from him.

Suddenly, the environment changed again, and he was seated amongst the other beings. The female entity advised that he was now part of their class and to pay attention to the teacher. There was a larger being at the front of the room and all beings listened intently. It spoke of universal law, a sort of code of ethics, and how the human species no longer followed this code. Ed looked at his companion and said, "There's something very trusting about you, loving, caring, wanting to help. I've never been through anything like this in my life." He continued to listen to the teacher and found that both his companion and the teacher spoke about "instability" on his planet including "eco-spiritual, and emotional instability." They told him, "Earth is shuddering in anguish, crying, weeping at the stupidity of humans losing contact with the inner soul of their being." Ed concentrated keenly and wondered what he could specifically do to help the situation. The female entity told him, "You have a chance. You have an inner sensitivity." Ed denied this, but she insisted. "You have a sensitivity. You pick up things. You can talk to the Earth. The Earth talks to you." Ed then recalled his fascination with nature; as a boy, he would go into the woods often and felt comfortable there. It felt familiar. The being continued, "You can hear the Earth. You can hear the anguish of the spirits. You can hear the wailing cries of the imbalances. It will save you." Ed felt caution at this point and asked what she meant by "save you." She explained to him that the Earth would repel those that did not work in "symbiotic harmony" with it. "The Earth's skin is going to swat some bugs off," she added.

Ed was mentally exhausted from all the information that he was given. And even though he listened intently and tried to truly understand, he felt frustrated due to the very nature of the abduction experience. He trusted the female being, but he had been forced into the situation. He calmed a bit and asked if he could write down the information that was given to him, but he was denied and told, "You will remember when you need to know."

During one of Ed's hypnosis sessions, he told Mack that he had a strict Catholic upbringing but that the thoughts and feelings the aliens had opened him up to felt frustratingly opposed to what his family valued, though he did agree with the beings. He explained, "She wired me into my emotions...she sort of gains either a clinical judgment of my emotional/mental typography, or gained my agreement." The doctor took him back to that night once again. With his eyes closed and his body relaxed, Ed was once again with the being.

She explained to him the "laws of the universe" and discussed with him politics, the Earth's environmental issues, the type of food humans consume, and violence against humanity. Ed felt a great deal of remorse for his past actions and was scared at what his species had become. After this encounter, he was open to change and different ideologies and expressed those ideas with friends and teachers. He felt out of place in the world, and his friends thought he had become strange. In his early adult life, he sought a relationship with someone with a similar outlook, someone he could relate to. He often found himself comparing women to the female entity. Eventually, he did meet someone with whom he shared those themes and after five years they married. Lynn, his wife, said, "I felt like I knew him already." He shared his encounter with her and she never doubted his story.

At the last hypnosis session, Mack asked Ed what he would do with this newfound knowledge, and he replied, "Too few will listen, but those that will listen and can work with the laws of nature, will survive to teach others on the other side…" Mack asked if humanity was lost; could it no longer be saved? Ed responded that no one could be saved now, it was too late, but once humans "crossed over," we would realize what we had done and would make better choices in our new plane of existence. Ed did offer one last thought to the doctor, saying, "Love is the key. Love and compassion for the Earth or the beings on the Earth…"

Ed and Lynn then decided that they would speak with other alien abduction experiencers and share the knowledge he had been given. Ed said that they would spend the rest of their time on this Earth advocating for the environment and helping humanity the best way that they could. Ed vowed to hold close his discussions with the female entity and to continue to learn from her every day. He no longer felt haunted by the experience, saying, "I don't find what happened to me traumatic… A great cloud, a shroud has been pulled away from my awareness…" He then concluded his sessions with Dr. Mack.

THE TOTE ROAD BOYS

The Passagassawakeag River is in Waldo County, Maine. It is sixteen miles long and flows southeast, Brooks to Belfast. The beauty of this stretch of water is not lost on the locals, as it is used year-round for fishing, canoeing, bird watching, boat races, snowmobiling, and ice fishing. At the east end of the river is an old area of Waldo County called Toad's End. This area is now mostly used for hiking and other summer recreation, but back in 1968, the kids called the area and road leading up to it the Tote Road. It was a private area, with power lines as long as the river stretched, where teenagers would gather to swim. Once fall settled in, the area became more of a party scene where young adults would meet up to talk, drink, and stargaze. The website UFO Casebook reported a peculiar series of events on Tote Road that started in October of 1968. A few teenage boys saw something among those stars—something that would change one young man's life forever.

The Tote Road in Waldo County, near Belfast, Maine.

Bill (pseudonym) was with his friends up on old Tote Road in the middle of October. He was still proud of the 1967 Ford that he'd bought by earning his own money all summer long. As Bill and his friends enjoyed the evening sky, they talked the night away. Unexpectedly, they all observed a star that seemed out of place. It was suspended in the sky lower than the others, then it quickly descended and hovered just above the power lines. As Bill explained, "We noticed a lighted object coming along approximately one hundred feet above the power line. The object came from the east and when a few hundred yards away from us, it halted still above the power lines." All occupants of Bill's vehicle were silent and stared at the oddity. Bill wrote, "We heard no sound...we saw the object spin about. It was of a basic, elliptical shape. It was lit with red and green lights and appeared to have windows." Things got even more strange when the UFO released tiny bright objects from underneath it. These objects seemed to float down and touch the power lines; no one observed the objects ascending back; they just disappeared. The boys watched this strange activity for about an hour until finally the UFO accelerated off to the west, leaving the teens alone, fascinated and frightened.

They sped off as well, but continued to talk about the encounter days later at school. They eventually made plans to go back out to Tote Road to see if they could witness the oddity again; Bill recounts, "This became a regular habit, and we went almost every night. About half the time, we were rewarded by seeing similar objects acting in much the same way as during our initial sighting. In fact, seeing these things became routine and we became desensitized to it. In time, we began to bring others with us to see the objects. On some nights, we would see multiple objects. Each one followed the power lines. Never did one deviate from this pattern."

On one November evening, Bill and his friend Samuel (pseudonym) were watching the UFO release its little lights when another, much larger object appeared above the first. The boys were startled and backed away slowly, headed toward their cars. They could see windows and watched the ship slowly rotate while it flashed red and blue lights. The object was so low and so large that they could actually see inside the strange aerial vehicle. Bill wrote, "We strained to see inside the windows but were unable to discern anything in any detail. We did see objects inside, but could not tell what they were." The giant craft acted like the first in releasing small, lighted objects toward the power lines. The boys felt conflicted—they were frightened at the behemoth UFO and eager to leave, but it was impossible for them to do so since they were fascinated by the spectacle before them. Then abruptly, all the objects sped off, even the small, floating lights released by the giant UFO. Once again, the boys found themselves alone, frightened and even more fascinated than before.

They continued with their nightly vigils in the area and took their dates there one evening. They parked in their usual spot and pulled out some alcohol refreshments that they'd brought with them. The friends chatted and drank a bit, and soon talk of the UFOs came up. Just as their conversation started, the massive object suddenly appeared in front of them and hovered over the power lines. Once again, it released the tiny bright lights as the girls stared in awe. Due to some liquid bravado and the adoring girls, Bill and Samuel were feeling particularly brave that night and got the idea to get out of the vehicle and go toward the object. Bill explained, "We decided to leave the car and walk down toward the object." Bill decided to hide their beer first; "Before leaving, we made sure to put our beer on the floor in back and I took off my coat and covered it, so anyone walking up to the car would not see it. We walked down toward the object and the girls became frightened and refused to go any further. So we stood there, watching this large object hover over the power lines. It was huge and the girls were speechless. This was the closest any of us had ever been to one of these. I was able to make out movement inside the craft, although again, the forms were vague and indistinct." Everyone felt exhausted from the exhilaration of the encounter and left the area before the UFOs did.

When Bill got up the next morning, he remembered his jacket in the car and went to retrieve it. He remembered covering the beer with it the night before, but when he looked in the back seat, his coat wasn't there. He looked under the seat, saw a sleeve of the coat, and pulled it out. Much to his surprise, it was only the sleeve! He said about the jacket, "This was a sheepskin-lined, corduroy coat, something like the Marlboro Man wore. And someone had pulled the arm off it … think it was the left arm. Little threads stuck out at different angles, which made me think that whoever did this was very strong." He kept thinking about the ruined jacket and assumed his friend Samuel was to blame, so he called him to discuss it. Their conversation escalated into an argument that went unresolved, and the group felt that Bill had overreacted. This led to everyone refusing to return to the Tote Road with Bill.

Despite being frightened, Bill couldn't help himself, so he went back—alone. As he pulled up to the parking area, he noticed something in the road. He thought it might be a dead animal, swerved his car around to avoid driving over it, and parked. He got out and looked back at the animal and realized he had been completely wrong. He ran over, knelt beside it, and picked it up in amazement. It was the rest of his coat! Seemingly dropped there from who knows where. A fresh dusting of snow had fallen, but no tire marks or footprints were present around the coat. Bill elaborated, "I was practically paralyzed with fear. I backed around and left as fast as I could. I have not been back to that place since, although I live only a few miles away." Bill went on to say that he brought the coat home and told his grandparents about everything—the objects big and little, the girls, the beer, and now ... the coat. His grandfather smirked, not believing a word Bill said. He grabbed the coat and used it as additional cushioning for their dog's bed. Immediately, the dog backed away and growled. His grandfather hollered at the dog to stop barking, but it would not until the coat was removed from the house. The grandfather looked at Bill with a hint of fear in his eyes; he then burned the coat and refused to speak about it.

Months turned into years. Bill and his friends graduated high school and the transition to adulthood began. Bill stayed behind and made a life for himself in Waldo County. Samuel joined the Marines and eventually moved out of state and lost touch with Bill. But years later, Samuel visited Maine with his family and looked up Bill to have a drink and talk about old times. Bill thought this would include a thrilling discussion about UFOs, but reported that Samuel "does not remember ever going to the Tote Road or seeing any UFOs back in 1968 or any other time." Bill was disappointed but didn't push the issue. He still thinks about those days; the '67 Ford, the girls, his pals, and of course the UFOs.

Bill did state that he is thinking of undergoing hypnotic regression therapy to try and elicit more information from his encounters. If he does, I hope it provides him with what he's looking for—perhaps acknowledgment of the events he and his friends observed, or maybe just closure to it all. Whatever it is, I wish him well.

A FAMILY'S ENCOUNTER

The state of Maine's first capital was the city of Portland, but in 1832 the location of the capital was changed to Augusta, as it was in a more centralized location. The Augusta area was first occupied by pioneers from the original Plymouth Colony in 1629. The Kennebec River served as the area's trading post for all types of agriculture, food, and other trades. Shortly after the city's establishment, a battle with Native Americans in the area started. They fought for what was rightfully theirs and were successful, causing the Plymouth Colony to sell the land in 1661 and then leave the area. The land lay dormant for over seventy-five years. Old legends speak of "star people" occupying the area throughout this time. Perhaps the following story, recorded by MUFON as Case 59680 and which I expand upon here, is a sign of this occurrence.

The Maine State House, circa 1800s. Courtesy of the Library of Congress.

The weather in Maine can be anything but predictable, and when fall starts to creep in, we hope the dog days of summer will stretch just a bit more. One Sunday evening in Augusta, in September of 2014, the weather was quite mild after a high of about 75 degrees that day. A family was traveling down Western Avenue after exiting the highway. They were headed home after a day of shopping, family visits, and dining, and all were tired. It was nearing 8:00 p.m., and three children with heavy eyes occupied the back seat. As their mother drove, she hoped to get them to bed soon, since school had just started for the year and she wanted them well rested.

"What the hell was that?" asked the father of the three children. Startled at his proclamation, his wife looked to where her husband pointed and saw exactly what he meant. He recounted what they saw: "We all noticed something hovering in the sky on the opposite side of the highway in front of us. It was triangular. It was not moving."

The kids stirred and sat up to see what Dad was getting all excited about. They too saw the hovering object and asked what it was. The dad could not provide an answer so they just continued staring, in awe. He then suggested that Mom pull the car over so they could get a better look. She knew better, declined his offer, and kept driving. Her husband studied every aspect of the triangular object that he could in the short amount of time it was observable. He wanted to capture the moment perfectly so he would be able to write about the experience later. His description is as follows: "At each vertex of the triangle, there was a white light. The three lights appeared equidistant from each other. We could see a flat bottom, and the light allowed us to see a 90-degree angle where the bottom met the edges that then moved up to give the object height." The object fascinated the family; even the kids did not seem scared and asked if it was from outer space. Dad shared a glance with Mom, eyebrows raised. "Most of us couldn't stop looking at the edges because they were not anything like any aircraft that we are familiar with. We could see that the object was a flat metal color. It had no shine to it. Where the light hit the object, it looked like a tin color. There were no color lights at all."

During the entire event, the object never moved, and eventually they lost sight of it as they continued the drive home. The witness wrapped up his description of the event with the statement, "We do not look for UFOs. This object was so out of place that it was difficult for us not to notice it."

The rest of the drive home was filled with discussions of UFOs, aliens, and military aircraft. All family members took turns providing explanations for the object. They laughed about Dad's initial reaction, but he and Mom shared a concerned look. They eventually arrived home and once the kids were settled, the parents went outside just to make sure the object hadn't followed them home. It hadn't, and they did not see anything else out of the ordinary that night. Even a couple of years after the encounter, whenever the subject of UFOs came up, they all shared a knowing glance.

10

IT WATCHED THEM
WHILE THEY SLEPT

One of the most vulnerable scenarios for anyone who owns a house or rents an apartment is the potential for a prowler to break in while you are sleeping. You're in a relaxed state and the last thought you should have while drifting off to sleep is of someone entering your home. But exactly this happened one night in June of 2011, when a couple from the Moosehead Lake region of Maine experienced an otherworldly intruder.

Paul and his wife Diane (pseudonyms) went to bed at around 11:00 p.m. In the early morning hours, Paul suddenly woke up and had an odd feeling that someone had just been in their bedroom. He sat up and looked around; the house was eerily silent. He slowly stood and looked out at the darkened hallway beyond the open bedroom door.

He looked back to the bed and saw his wife asleep, unbothered by whatever phantom disturbance had woken him.

He walked without sound as he entered the hallway. He crept past the second bedroom, beyond the bathroom, and stood at the top of the stairs. He peered down the stairwell, hesitant to descend. He sighed deeply and inched down the stairs. Upon reaching the living room, he felt an onslaught of goose bumps ripple the skin on his forearms. He rubbed them methodically as he walked to the front door to double check that it was locked. He then approached a nearby window but saw nothing out of the ordinary and continued to the kitchen. Again, nothing was out of place. He scanned the basement door for a moment, reluctant to check the darkened bowels of the house, and opted it out of his security detail. On his way back to the stairs, he checked the front door again, and finally felt satisfied that it was locked.

The next morning, Diane noticed the dark circles under Paul's eyes and asked, "Did you sleep okay, hon?" He looked at her for a moment, reluctant to tell her, but finally said, "I woke up in the middle of the night. I could swear someone had been in the house. I looked all over." "You think we got a ghost?" she said, laughing. He laughed with her, but in the back of his mind he knew something out of the ordinary had happened.

Weeks went by without incident, but then one night, Paul woke up again. He had that same feeling from the first night and immediately sat up, looking for an explanation.

He retraced his previous steps and when he looked out the window, he briefly observed the essence of a bright light from somewhere above, but it quickly faded. He unlocked the front door and stepped out hurriedly to find the source of the light, but found nothing.

He went back to bed, and while he was pulling the covers back over himself, his wife suddenly spoke. "What happened? Did you go outside?" He jumped at the sound of her voice, as he thought she was asleep, and the two shared a laugh over his startled reaction. Paul explained that he had woken up again and felt that someone had been in the house. He also explained the odd light and that he had gone outside to see what it was, but it was gone by the time he got out there. "You were probably just dreaming," his wife offered and lay back down. Paul knew that he hadn't been dreaming and could not shake the ominous feeling of the whole thing.

During the weekend, he unpacked his camera and brought it upstairs. He was not exactly sure why he did this, but knew he needed it close by. Paul was also an amateur astronomer and had a telescope set up in an upstairs bedroom. He kept it pointed out of an east-facing window due to its unobstructed view of the sky. Their home was adjacent to Moosehead Lake and he often enjoyed utilizing the device to scan the cosmos. He placed the camera on his nightstand, and when he turned in that evening, he felt a sense of unexplained confidence with it being near him.

As time went on, Paul slept soundly. He continued with his nightly security checks but did not have a repeat of the previous incidents. A few weeks later, as the couple were getting ready for bed, Diane noticed a bright light outside their window and called her husband over. "What the hell is that?" she asked. "I bet it's that light I saw!" Paul moved her aside lovingly and peered out the window. He saw a "bright star-like object," and both observed it hovering for a moment and then watched it move in what they described as "random directions." The window was close to Paul's nightstand and he slowly reached for the camera. He treated the light as you would a wild animal you were trying to photograph, not wanting to scare it off. But without warning the object disappeared, and Paul was understandably frustrated. Over the next month, he and his wife observed the light numerous times, but it always eluded the watchful eye of his camera.

During a late August evening, they observed the light once more. It appeared different than before, and it was closer. As reported on the *World UFO Photos and News* website, Paul said that "the object appeared square and was larger, subtending an angle equal to a dime at arms-length." He reflexively reached for his camera, slowly moved it toward the widow frame, and was finally able to procure a picture. He recounted, "I was able to photograph the object moving about with a 200 mm zoom lens, resting the camera on the window frame. No detailed information can be extracted from the images due to movement artifact, but expansive movement over a period of about 30 minutes is documented. The area of sky in which these observations have been made is northwest of our location."

After he photographed the object, the light ceased its visits to their home and Paul stopped experiencing the odd feeling of someone entering their bedroom. He thought that perhaps the photograph was some sort of closure to the experience. But soon after, he began having memories of previous sightings of lights in the sky around his home. Paul explained, "Several years ago involved a very bright object, moving at a tremendous speed, from west to east across the lake, essentially going from horizon to horizon in seconds. No sound heard. No colored lights." At the time, he certainly thought it odd but quickly forgot about the incident. Then in 2009, two years before the latest series of events, he saw another light. "I was up on a ridge behind our camp with the telescope. While doing a bright star alignment, I noted a bright, disc-shaped object suddenly becoming visible over the western drop-off. Because of the elevation, I thought at first that I was seeing a plane with its landing lights on. However, this object stayed in the same position for several minutes then just winked out."

Paul and Diane have not reported on any further encounters since 2011, and it is thought they have stopped altogether. Despite this, I can just imagine Paul conducting nightly security detail, triple-checking the front door to make sure that it's locked. I can see Diane looking at him thankfully and not scoffing at the idea of an invisible intruder. Even though they have not commented further about the incident, they did publicly share the photo that Paul took. It can be viewed by doing a Google Image search for "Lily Bay Township UFO."

11

THE CREATURE ON WASHINGTON STREET

The first time I heard about Mothman was from a 1997 episode of the television show *The X-Files*. Entitled "Detour," it was one of the series's self-contained "monster of the week" storylines. Even though I preferred the show's UFO/alien story arc, this episode was monumentally fantastic. It showed the quintessential odd couple in all their glory. The tale combined the perfect balance of humor and masterfully scary elements, and it remains one of my favorites to this day. The plot featured two terrifying monsters that could camouflage themselves, which allowed for them to hide in plain sight. Tension built throughout the episode, and there was just no way to prepare for the "jump scenes" even if you knew when they were about to occur. I remember reading an article somewhere that described the episode as if Stephen King had written a "made for TV" *Predator* movie.

Mothman Origins

The creatures from *The X-Files* episode bore no resemblance to the actual mysterious figure sighted in Point Pleasant, West Virginia, during a thirteen-month period that started in 1966. But in the show, Mulder mentioned that the creatures could be related to the Mothman because of their seemingly supernatural tendencies. It wasn't until about five years after the episode aired that there was an explosion of Mothman popularity due to the release of the movie *The Mothman Prophecies*. The movie was based off John Keel's book of the same name, and took numerous liberties in its vast discrepancies from the book. Regardless, the movie did manage to convey the whimsical, odd, and downright macabre atmosphere the book had created. Furthermore, while not the best representation of Keel's work, the movie did bring many people, including myself, to the enigmatic, true-life events surrounding Mothman in West Virginia. I immediately rushed out to get Keel's book, but found it had been out of print for quite some time. However, not long after the movie came out, a new edition was published using the movie's art as its cover (I hate when that happens). No matter; I had to have it. I must have read that copy over one hundred times (not really, but a lot). Other publications about Mothman came out that year as well, including Loren Coleman's *Mothman and Other Curious Encounters*. A British paranormal magazine called *Fortean Times* released a special Mothman edition. Again, I had to have both of these, and both I had. (Mr. Coleman signed my copy of his book when I first met him in Prospect, Maine, at the Paranormal Fair hosted by Friends of Fort Knox in 2009).

The story of Mothman and the townspeople of Point Pleasant is a measureless and complex series of otherworldly and cryptid events. The thirteen-month ordeal started in November of 1966 and culminated with the devastating collapse of the town's main bridge, which resulted in the deaths of forty-six people. John Keel, along with his "Scully," local journalist Mary Hyre, investigated encounters, interviewed witnesses, and experienced their own strange happenings throughout that time frame. Both journalists sighted UFOs, Mary had encounters with a "man in black," and John received odd phone calls from a peculiar man who called himself Indrid Cold. The abstract of the book describes it this way: "A journalist recounts his investigation of a bizarre winged apparition, mysterious lights in the sky, mutilation deaths of domestic animals, and other eerie and unexplained events in Point Pleasant, West Virginia." I haven't even begun to scratch the surface of Mothman in Point Pleasant, so I would encourage you to read Keel's work on the events that transpired. You can find a copy in almost every mom-and-pop bookstore, and of course from online book sources as well.

One of the more famous encounters occurred on November 15, 1966. The story is of two young married couples who were driving in a part of Point Pleasant called "the TNT area." The place was once used as a munitions plant during World War II but had since turned into the local teenage hangout. Mary Hyre posed the following question in her article about the incident: "What stands six feet tall, has wings, two big red eyes six inches apart, and glides along behind an auto at 100 miles an hour?" With this question, she referenced the description of the creature the witnesses had observed. They had certainly seen something odd that night.

Almost thirty-five years later to the month, a man saw something similar in October of 2001. He was not in West Virginia; he was living in the beautiful coastal town of Camden, Maine.

"What caught me was the wings..."

Finding the full story of the Maine man's encounter was difficult at first. Most of my research only unearthed short descriptions that lacked significant detail. Fellow author and friend Michelle Souliere helped out by tracking a bit more to the story and uncovering a name for the witness. I located the gentleman on Facebook in May of 2017 and contacted him about the encounter. He was open to sharing the entirety of the events; a pseudonym has been used by request.

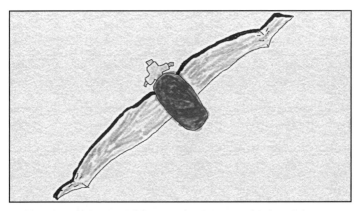

The witness's drawing of the creature. Courtesy of Robert Osbourne.

This incredible tale began when Camden resident Robert Osbourne walked down Washington Street at around 6:00 p.m. on an early evening in October of 2001. As he walked toward his apartment, he heard a squeaking sound coming from somewhere nearby. I asked him to elaborate, and he said, "I heard this very distinct squeak. I thought it was a rodent of some sort, but it surprised me because it was so loud and clear. I thought it must be right underfoot or in front of me." As he looked for the source of the sound he was startled to see a large, humanoid shape fly above him. "It was a roundish body with long, translucent wings, and what I could have sworn was a funny-looking head (small and weird ... like it was a nub with tubes on it?). I can't say I got a good look at that. What caught me was the wings, which were very, very long. Even at that age (seventeen years old), I knew enough about the wildlife in the area and was not familiar with any local animals that had wings like that (outside of bats), but this was way too big for that." Osbourne was wholly bewildered by the uncanny sight and watched as it flew low, near his home. "Its wings sort of … fluttered a little," he told me. "But just sort of like it was moving the tips, and it tilted and flew over the house, into the woods and swamps out behind it. It passed right over the eaves, where my apartment was, so I got a perfect comparison for wing-span, and that thing stretched easily from edge to edge of the slant. Definitely over 24–25 feet." The sighting confused Osbourne; he knew that it was clearly mammalian, but felt that it couldn't be real. (I visited the location in June of 2017, and the eave was easily twenty-five feet across.)

Osbourne thought about the encounter often, and shared his experience with some friends and family. Most dismissed the being he'd seen as a large bird, but he knew that what he saw was entirely different. "I've seen big birds," he said. "I've seen huge turkey buzzards before, and since then I've seen all sorts of wildlife in this state and others, I've never seen anything like this." He wanted to share his experience, or at the very least have it logged somehow. He reached out to *Cryptozoology.com* (the website is now revamped as a Facebook presence) to share his story. His post sat dormant for years. Various reports and webpages would cite the encounter as

"Mothman seen in Camden, Maine" but lacked a connection back to Osbourne's original story.

A few months later, Osbourne was again walking on Washington Street and saw the figure once more! It was much farther away this time. "I was walking up Washington Street from downtown," he recalled, "and as I crested the top of the hill I looked down towards the house, [and] I saw the thing again! It did a near identical maneuver, sweeping across the street and pivoting up into the swamps and woods behind the houses. It didn't fly as low as last time, and I didn't hear it, but I saw it. Now, this was a distance away from the previous sighting, probably a good three hundred feet." Osbourne doubted size in his first sighting, and now believed the large bird theory that others used to explain his first encounter. So during the second sighting, he thought, "Well, I probably just saw a big bird."

He thought little of his most recent encounter, went on with life, and eventually enrolled into college. A couple of years went by without incident, and in the summer of 2003 he returned to Camden on a summer break from school. One midafternoon, he got together with an old friend and the pair drove around town. During their drive, an odd occurrence took place that reminded him of the creature he'd seen before. As Osbourne explained, "I'm driving through town with a friend, and we're just enjoying the weather. We're down in a section of town I don't usually go to, and I didn't mean to go out that way, we were just puttering around. Well, we're driving along, when out of nowhere we hit something. It smacked into the windshield, and we came to a stop. Both of us thought it was a papier-mâché or something like that. It was sorta gray, lumpy, and vaguely translucent on the wings." Stunned, the pair sat in the car and just stared at the oddity. It splayed across the windshield, seemingly deceased. As the car rolled to a stop the creature suddenly came to life and flew off! Osbourne and his friend were confounded, and both admitted to having an eerie feeling they couldn't quite explain during the event. That feeling, coupled with the translucent wings, brought Osbourne back to that first encounter, and he was not as dismissive of the events any longer.

Also, a concurrent theme for Osbourne was a reoccurring dream he had. In the dream, he found himself back on Washington Street, in the same spot as his first encounter. While he stood on the street, he suddenly realized that an object was overhead, and he looked up to see a large UFO hovering silently. He told me, "I actually had a repetitive dream for a bit about walking back home at night across town, stopping at that stop, looking up, and realizing there was a floating house above me. Then it lights up suddenly and makes a horrible noise, and I wake up." I expressed to Osbourne that it could simply be a UFO dream, but perhaps it was a repressed memory. He agreed with the latter.

Notably, Keel wrote about concurrent happenings in Point Pleasant, West Virginia, during the Mothman sightings. These included numerous reports of UFOs and men-in-black encounters.

About a year after his third encounter with the strange bird creature, Osbourne was back in Camden again visiting his girlfriend. One evening, they sat outside together and watched the sky, since the aurora borealis was visible on that rare night. Later, the pair heard squeak-like sounds that were all too familiar to Osbourne. The sounds emanated from the nearby woods that he'd seen the creature fly into that first time. His girlfriend mostly ignored the squeaks, but he knew better and looked toward the woods, knowing it was near. He said to me, "We both heard that high-pitched squeaking noise coming from the far woods across from the field. It would be the same patch of marshes and woods that ran behind my house where I kept seeing the thing. My girlfriend (now wife) is from Boston, so she just assumed it was bats or deer or whatever we have up here, but it sounded exactly like that damn thing again. We heard it a few different times that night."

It's been years since Osbourne has been witness to anything quite as strange as the winged figure. He lives in Wells, Maine, now, and oddly enough, right next to a marshy area. When I asked him if he still thinks about the creature, he said, "I can actually still picture it in my head perfectly." He still wonders what the being could have been. I mentioned Mothman, and he said, "I've occasionally wondered if it was something like that. Keel used the term 'ultraterrestrial,' and I'm inclined to think it was that. I've often called it the 'big birdie' when I've thought about it, but I don't think it was a bird or anything like one really."

And what about the dreams of the UFOs? Osbourne did mention that reoccurring dreams had recently started up again. He stated, "I did have a series of weird repeating dreams last year about walking into my bathroom, looking out the window, and seeing a disc just over the tree line. Then I'd wake up. I really didn't give it much thought for some reason … we had just moved into the new house, and we had so much on our plates, I guess I just put it aside."

Could Osbourne be a beacon for such strange phenomena? Maybe it *was* just a large bird he saw; the sandhill crane is large and seen in parts of the state. Or perhaps he was at the right place at the right time when he sighted the creature on Washington Street. And the UFO dreams—well maybe that is all they are. Despite this, he is adamant that he saw something peculiar during those encounters. I'd like to think that a version of the Mothman occasionally enjoys the salty air of Camden, Maine.

Investigating the Mothman of Knox County

On June 22, 2017, I accompanied my lovely family to the beautiful Camden Riverhouse Motel. It is situated right in the heart of downtown Camden and is approximately a two-minute drive from where the creature was sighted. On our first day in town, we enjoyed a walk around the grounds of the library, we took the kiddo to the high school so he could skateboard, and we went for a swim in the hotel's indoor pool (rain was in the forecast). As night fell, I quietly planned for my evening investigation. I went to the car to check my gear, which included a flashlight and night vision camera. What? I've never investigated Mothman before, what else would I need?

Anyway, I kissed my goodbyes and drove to the police station. I explained to a friendly officer my intentions to look for the elusive beast in the areas off Washington Street. Some of the areas do not allow visitors after 10:00 p.m., and I wanted to make sure I had their blessing. He granted me permission, and I was off. First stop: Shirt Tail Point Park. Time: 11:30 p.m. By day, Shirt Tail is a small but gorgeous family swimming area with picnic tables, one rustic hibachi grill, and shallow waters. By night, the area changes into a creep-filled breeding ground for unnamed ghouls.

Washington Street sign in Camden, Maine.

Shirt Tail Point area of Camden, Maine.

Oh, is that just me? Well, I'm never one to shy away from an investigation, so I parked my car, shut off the lights, and stepped outside. A bench sat about ten feet in front of the water on a grassy area. I sat quietly and listened. From time to time, I would do a scan of the area with my night vision camera but saw nothing out of the ordinary.

After about an hour, I decided to take a drive up Washington Street. I drove in silence while I waited for the Mothman to dive-bomb my car like in that scene from *The Mothman Prophecies* when Debra Messing crashes her car.

The marshy area behind the apartment near the sighting.

It never happened, so back to Shirt Tail I went. I sat once more on the bench and observed some mist rolling in as the weather started to turn. After about three hours, I called it a night and headed back to the quaint hotel room that housed my loves. Time: 2:30 a.m.

After arriving back to the room, I went through the pictures I'd taken and continued working on this book. I had one more night in the area, so I planned another outing. This time, I had a guest investigator with me—my son! This eleven-year-old (at the time) boy is the kindest soul you'd ever meet, and he went with me in the afternoon to scout for a new location. I found a marshy area situated roughly behind the apartment of the first sighting, and saw that it had ample parking away from the sights and sounds of the main road. At around 10:30 p.m., the crypto-kid and I headed out again and drove to the location. We sat in the dark as the kiddo munched on some Sour

Patch Kids. I explained the story of the Point Pleasant Moth-man to him, he asked some great questions about its authenticity, and we watched a trailer to the movie.

After a little while, we both got out of the car to listen for anything walking in the marshy area or the woods beyond it. We heard a lot. Most likely deer (there's a ton in the area); however, the kiddo did see some odd movement and a glowing red light from deep within the woods. He said, "It's like its watching us. I can see it come and go. See!" Just then he pointed out a glowing red light (for about the fifth time or so), but I finally saw it for myself this time. It was fleeting, but certainly out of place in relation to the area that we were in. With that said, it truly could have been the glow of brake lights from a car, given that we are not familiar with the area and an unknown road could have been closer than we thought. We took pictures, and pareidolia (when the mind makes familiar patterns when nothing is there) was on max—we saw faces and shapes in the pixilation.

After a time, I took him over to Shirt Tail and we sat in the car with the lights off and the windows down. We kept hearing something walking in the water; it was just far off enough in the darkness that we were unable to see it. I did turn on the headlights a few times, but the source of the phantom walker eluded us. It was probably a deer.

After a couple of hours, tired and ready for bed, we headed back to the hotel room. The kiddo fell fast asleep as I went through the pictures again with *The Golden Girls* television show on in the background. I yawned loudly, and my eyes watered afterwards. I took that as my cue to turn in. Despite a valiant effort, and some excellent company on my second night, the Creature from Washington Street remained hidden. Rest well, old boy. I'll be back.

BEHOLD THE OTHERWORLDLY EVIDENCE

Let's face it, there have been hundreds of thousands of UFOs captured on video—some more authentic than others, and some more famous than others. There are the Phoenix Lights from 1997, numerous video feeds from the International Space Station, the White Sands crash, the 2004 Mexico UFO Fleet recorded by an air patrol team searching for drug smugglers... whew! And others—the fascinating Graaff-Reinet video from 1998; the 2008 videos from Istanbul, Turkey, which are still causing controversy to this day; and one of the more recent viral videos—the 2011 Jerusalem "Dome of the Rock" UFO. It was initially debunked as a CGI hoax until a second video emerged from the same night, from a different angle, which made it harder to debunk.

We have some great videos of unidentified flying objects in Maine, as well. I invite you to take this book to your laptop or smartphone right now and check out these videos. Scrutinize them and decide for yourself what they could be. Some are more convincing than others, and I most certainly welcome your thoughts.

The Buxton Lights:
Buxton, Maine, December 19, 2016

YouTube, Video Titled
"Possible UFO over Buxton, Maine USA?"

James (pseydonym) was home in his bedroom one winter evening, just six days before Christmas of 2016. He saw a light in the sky in his peripheral vision and turned to see what it was. He saw one light, then another—that's when he grabbed his cell phone to capture the lights on video. Radio station Q97.9 (WJBQ) reported James as stating, "I saw a second one a minute later, so I grabbed my phone and caught this. Winds at the time were blowing SSW. These were heading east, eliminating Chinese lanterns. It lasted just over a minute."

What James captured is nothing short of amazing: a string of lights in the sky seemingly just switched on. It seems almost too good to be true. But that has not swayed

James in any way. He stands by his video and says, "Skeptics welcome, we are all entitled to our opinions." And boy, have they come forward, especially since he provided the video to the YouTube channel "SecureTeam10," whose videos are often described as dubious in nature.

An anonymous source told me that James did not report the sighting to MUFON or NUFORC. This was due to the fact, as James explained to my source, that those agencies have been "compromised." He also claimed that a sheriff in the area saw the lights that night but was afraid to come forward. According to MUFON's State Director for Maine, Valerie Schultz, a couple of reports did come in that night, but she could not say if any were from James.

I contacted James at the end of December 2016 to discuss the matter and we agreed to talk after the holidays. Unfortunately, he never returned any of my follow-up messages. Regardless of the controversy, I urge you to check out his video (location and name given at top of this section). It's fascinating, and I would love to know your thoughts. Do you think it's genuine? Is it a possible hoax? Decide for yourself and let me know.

Viral Video: Cumberland, Maine, July 4, 2016

DailyMotion.com, Video Titled "Case 77585—
Cumberland County, Maine—July 4, 2016"

After dinner and fireworks, a family sat at home, happy with how the evening's events had unfolded. While getting up to go to another room, a woman noticed an out-of-place light in the sky when they passed a window. She called for the rest of the family to see the oddity, and the husband described the encounter to MUFON as follows: "My wife looked out the window and saw an object with bright lights high in the sky. We thought the object could be a sophisticated large drone, possibly military. However, when we reviewed the video at the end, frame by frame, it appears to spin and then disappear." (As a UFO researcher, I appreciate that the family did not immediately jump to conclusions and first considered their sighting as a possible drone.) The husband goes on to say, "The object hovered stationary for several minutes. Using my HD video camera zoomed in at 60x I could see an A frame shape for each structure, a red and green light in the middle, and three bright white lights on top. It began spinning and then disappeared as shown frame by frame on the video." The video was submitted to MUFON for analysis.

Another Viral Video: Rockland, Maine, June 14, 2015

YouTube, Video Titled "UFO Triangle, Coastal Maine"

Tyler Pendleton, a resident of Rockland, recorded a peculiar video one evening in June of 2015. At around 9:00 p.m., Tyler noticed some odd lights grouped together in the sky. They were in a triangle formation, and when he approached the window, he could not hear any sound emanating from them. He pulled out his cell phone and recorded the peculiar sight, a photo of which appeared in the *PenBay Pilot*. He told the newspaper, "I even called local airports at Owls Head and Bangor, asked if they had any record of anything flying in that formation and they said they didn't."

The video of Tyler's encounter soon went viral on social media. WCSH Channel 6 reported that the director of the Astronomy Center at the University of Maine, Scott Mitchell, said that "there could be any number of explanations, just the weather here on Earth can get kinda crazy, so it could be any number of things … "

In my opinion, after watching this video, there is absolutely no way to confuse the lights with a weather phenomenon.

Bigfoot and UFOs—
The Michael Merchant Tapes

YouTube, Video Titled "Shocking UFO
eye witness account Wytopitlock Maine"

Michael Merchant is a Maine native and biologist who made appearances on cable television shows such as *The $10 Million Bigfoot Bounty* and Discovery Channel's *Out of the Wild: Venezuela.* He also has a YouTube channel called "SnowWalkerPrime," where he posts videos dedicated to the pursuit of Bigfoot, albeit humorously. He categorizes his videos as entertainment, yet he does share some intriguing tales about Bigfoot, UFO sightings, and other creatures.

One video tells the story of him and someone identified as "Lady K" being out in the Haynesville Woods conducting wildlife survey work. Night fell fast, and the couple decided to camp in a gravel pit on the logging road in the area. They lay there watching the sky for quite some time. They noticed airplanes, shooting stars, meteors, and satellites. Then, as Michael explained, an odd meteor entered his field of view: "It was substantially large, it was just a ball of flames. It then just goes into slow motion." Lady K added, "It slowed down to the speeds, pretty much what the satellites look like, just gently going."

They observed the light change directions as it began following a plane that was in the area. It made no sound, though they could hear the airplane quite easily. They beamed their flashlight in the direction of the object, after which it increased its speed and left the area. Later that same night, they were disturbed by something hiding in the woods. Michael explained, "It was as if something was up there patrolling the edge of that gravel pit all night long, when we're not looking, and when we'd get up to look, it stopped."

If you would like to check out some fun (mostly meant for entertainment purposes), do a search on YouTube for SnowWalkerPrime.

Bright Light: Bangor, Maine, August 25, 2013

DailyMotion.com, Video Titled "UFO flying
over Bangor, Maine 25 August 2013"

Sky-watching has become a normal part of life for some residents in Maine. From the northern lights to meteor showers to shooting stars, the pristine sky in this area of the world could be considered unmatched.

One such sky-watcher had his eyes and camera pointed up as he recorded something he could not quite explain. When he reported it to MUFON, the witness explained, "I looked up and saw a close, low-flying, intense, bright lighted object and notice there was no sound. It was moving from S to N-NW. I began recording with the camera and was eventually able to stabilize it on a tripod and record it moving low across the sky."

He eventually lost sight of the object as it disappeared behind a tree line. He walked his land to a spot where he had an open view of the night sky, and found it! He continued recording as it hovered over the Kenduskeag River: "It flew low and hovered silently and steadily in the sky at approx. 30 degrees, just over the power lines, trees, and eventually hovered over the river for approx. two minutes."

While the video is of low quality, the object is, in my opinion, quite obviously not an airplane.

The Star Wars UFO:
Bangor, Maine, October 1, 2013

YouTube, Video Titled "Strange UFO hovered over
Bangor ME, USA on 10/01/2013 (Close Up)"

Okay, this is one of those too-good-to-be-true UFO sightings that one only dreams of capturing on video. This is a daytime sighting, great quality, and looks as though it could be straight out of a Star Wars movie. The story goes that a young gentleman is out taking his dog for a walk. He noticed at one point that the dog had become agitated, and that's when something in the sky caught his attention. He fumbled for his cell phone and caught something quite phenomenal. Give it a watch—several, if you will. This may be just too good to be true (definitely).

Comparing the Videos

Did you watch all the viral videos? What did you think? The first one looked to me like a drone. Valerie Schultz at MUFON submitted the video for analysis, and it has come back as "authentic." Authentic in this case means that there was no tampering done to the video, including CGI. However, that still does not discount the drone theory. The second viral video is much more convincing to me, and what's odd is how the lights kept their distance perfectly from one another.

I encourage you to seek out more UFO videos—they are out there. I equally encourage you to take your own! You never know what you might find. If you catch something, look me up on Facebook at "Nomar Slevik Author" and send me a message. I'd love to talk to you about it!

CLOSE ENCOUNTERS

By MUFON's Valerie Schultz

During the early morning hours of December 10, 2016, a large and silent craft was observed moving slowly northeast over southern Maine. Two separate cases about this sighting were reported to MUFON.

It Was the Size of a Football Stadium!

According to testimony in MUFON Case #80969, the witness explained that his location on a mountaintop in East Baldwin offered him a perfect panoramic view of the area. The witness recalled that "December 10, 2016, was a clear night with no moonlight and no clouds. I was outside at 4:30 a.m. with my German Shepherds when I observed three craft flying towards me from just under Orion's Belt. I thought they were military as I heard the roaring of what sounded like an old 1960s jet engine at full throttle. As the craft got closer, I saw that there were two smaller escorts and one giant craft/object in the middle that was the size of a football stadium! The three crafts approached from the West then changed direction to head Northeast. They were perfectly aligned in formation traveling over five hundred feet in altitude but alarmingly low. I realized they were in some kind of force field that obstructed the clear view of the center, giant craft. Stars were obscured all around the force field for hundreds of yards. The rear end had a rounded look to it that was glowing a strange yellow color. The front was somewhat curved but it was the size that was so impressive. There were three reddish orange lights in the front of the craft."

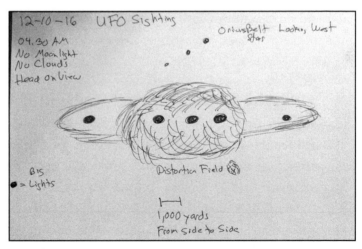

A witness drawing with the distortion field. Courtesy of MUFON.

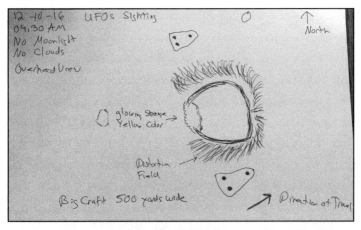

A witness drawing with the direction of travel. Courtesy of MUFON.

The witness was not entirely sure of the shape of the giant craft because of the force field surrounding it. However, he said it was "shaped and sized like a football stadium with great height, width, and depth, but no noise."

The escorts were in triangular shape similar to a TR-3B craft. They each had "one red light up front and two red lights in the rear at the base of the triangle."

The witness was surprised at the sound that he heard coming from the escorts. He explained that when all three crafts were overhead there was no sound. But when the three crafts were approaching and then again after the craft had passed, the witness heard a strange sound. This sound seemed too loud and too constant, which led the witness to believe that the sound was artificial.

Another peculiar piece to this encounter is that during the sighting the witness reported feeling ill. "As the formation approached, I was hit with a wave of nausea, felt anxiety, and fear. One of my K-9s ran off back to the house and the other cowered behind me. Both have been agitated ever since and hesitant to go out at night." When asked how long the illness lasted, the witness described that he felt chronically fatigued and had aches in his joints for a month. He also said that he developed a post-traumatic (PTSD) feeling whenever he heard a jet overhead and speculated that he had symptoms of radiation poisoning. His dogs did not have any physical sickness, but they too become anxious when hearing the roar of a jet's engine. This also lasted for about a month afterwards.

The duration of this sighting was five minutes and he estimated the three crafts' speed at around 200 miles per hour. When we spoke of the altitude of the craft, the witness replied, "My house is at one thousand feet and I would estimate the three crafts were two to three thousand feet above me." The witness followed up by stating that their altitude was well under five thousand feet and added, "It was just so startling to see such craft so low and so close." The witness submitted a drawing of the event.

It Moved Effortlessly
like a Boat through Water

Meanwhile, at 4:44 a.m. on December 10, 2016—fourteen minutes later, in Windsor (sixty-three miles northeast of East Baldwin)—a man was driving his wife to work on Route 17. She observed a large object outside her car window and asked her husband to pull over. According to testimony in MUFON Case #80908, the witness said, "I stopped the vehicle to see for myself. It was large and shaped like a carpenter's framing square, triangle shaped, at least 6 red lights and a weird turquoise light that went off at its point. It was silent."

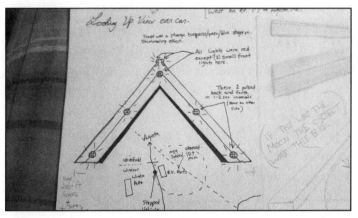

A witness drawing of their view from a car. Courtesy of MUFON.

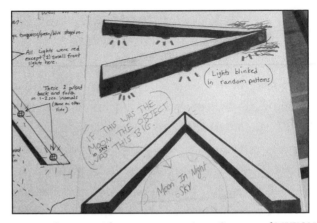

A witness drawing with a moon comparison. Courtesy of MUFON.

The craft was described as two to three times the size of the moon, and the witness watched as the craft traveled slowly over high tension power lines. The altitude was reported to be about two hundred to three hundred feet. This witness also submitted a drawing of the sighting and added, "It wasn't your normal plane. I could not believe the size of it."

When asked about the speed of the silent craft, the witness replied, "It's difficult to explain, like a satellite, but not as quick. Like a jumbo jet when it comes in for a landing, but a bit slower. It was slow enough to where we could make out some detail, but fast enough to where it was out of our sight within ten minutes or so."

It seemed to the witness that there was some sort of force field around the craft. He described it as "shimmering similar to road heat on a hot day. The craft was effortlessly moving like a boat through water, floating with no resistance." They also reported that the huge craft was silent, but after the craft had passed them, a "strange rumble sound" was heard.

Like the East Baldwin witness, both the husband and wife became nauseous when observing the craft. The wife continued on to work after the sighting and "struggled that day with the nausea and vomiting." The husband felt nauseous for a few hours after, but the wife's illness lasted for three days.

Along with a detailed drawing of what they observed, the Windsor witnesses submitted a short video of the sighting. Analysis of the video was performed by MUFON's Director of Research, Robert Powell, who broke it down into individual frames. By doing so, Mr. Powell was able to observe stars in the video's background. The stars provided us with a frame of reference to observe the object's movement. The object in the video was stationary during the few seconds it was visible.

Comparing the Two Cases

MUFON Cases #80969 and #80908 have several similarities in their descriptions. The first witness, in East Baldwin, observed a football stadium sized craft (with two triangular escorts) approach from the west and travel northeast at 4:30 a.m. on December 10, 2016. The second case, #80908 from Windsor, occurred fourteen minutes later, at 4:44 a.m., and also traveled northeast. Both witnesses reported the crafts were traveling around 200 to 300 miles per hour. Using the formula *speed = distance divided by time* or *63 miles ÷ 14 minutes*, the average speed would equal 4.5 miles per minute. If you then convert the miles per minute to miles per hour—*60 x 4.5*—then the resulting speed of the craft would equal 270 mph. This clearly correlates with witness testimony about the crafts' speed. When compared with the typical speed of a commercial airliner, which travels between 546 and 575 mph, 270 mph is noticeably slower.

When we compared accounts of the shape of the large craft, we discovered that the East Baldwin witness found it difficult to discern due to a field that distorted it and blurred out stars. The front of the craft seemed round and had three big reddish-orange headlights. The rear also seemed round and had a yellow glow. The Windsor witnesses observed a large, triangular-shaped object, which they compared to a carpenter's framing square (triangle shape with two sides coming to a point in the front). On each side of the craft they observed two red lights that pulsed back and forth in one- to two-second intervals, with another red light at the front point. There were also two smaller lights on the front tip with a turquoise/green/blue color that had a shimmering effect, and did not blink. The shape descriptions are different; however, both cases mentioned some type of distortion field around the object that gave a wavy, slightly obscured appearance to the sky. The Windsor witnesses described the craft "floating with no resistance like a boat going through water." They also noticed a shimmering effect coming from the craft like road heat on a hot day.

In both cases, the witnesses described the large craft as silent when it passed overhead. The East Baldwin witness heard a strange and possibly artificial jet sound as the three crafts approached, and then again after they passed, but it was silent when they were overhead. Again, this is similar to the Windsor witness who heard a "strange rumble sound" after the craft passed.

Witnesses from both cases reported feeling ill as they observed the craft. The East Baldwin witness was hit with a wave of nausea as the three crafts approached. He, along with his dogs, became anxious and fearful, which lasted for a month. The Windsor witnesses both became nauseous while observing the craft and for a few days after.

When speaking with the witnesses in these two intriguing cases, they both come across as extremely credible. Also, it is quite clear that they witnessed something highly unusual in the early hours of December 10, 2016. An interesting point to note is that the Windsor witnesses observed the large, silent craft travel over high-tension power lines, seemingly following them as the craft slowly traveled northeast into interior Maine (refer to "The Tote Road Boys" story earlier in this book for similarities in power line interest from UFOs). An important connection between the cases is that all three witnesses became ill with nausea as they watched the large craft. All three witnesses were concerned about the health effects that they encountered while observing this low-flying unidentified craft, and the East Baldwin witness mentioned that "there were an unusual number of ambulance calls in the area for anxiety or heart attacks the following day."

MUFON Case #80969 was investigated and closed as "Unknown" by Field Investigator Fred Richards and by me, as State Director for Maine. MUFON Case #80908 was investigated and closed as "Unknown" by me.

TRAPPERS
IN ATHENS

**By Erik Cooley, MUFON's Valerie Schultz,
and Nomar Slevik**

Trapping—wherein animals are trapped for their fur and sold for livable wages—has been a tradition in Maine even before the state was established. Previous to 1947, the state's legislature set the trapping season length; however, Maine trappers begrudged the short amount of time granted. This changed with the creation of the Maine Trappers Association in 1947, and the organization was able to extend the season's allotment of time. The Trappers Association is still intact and holds various conventions and weekend outings throughout the year.

In 1988, one such weekend outing occurred in the small town of Athens. This blue-collar agricultural town was named after the famous Greek city, and as of the 2010 census, it's home to a little over one thousand people (I have more Facebook likes than this place; that's small!). Athens was one of the first incorporated towns in the area (1804) and sits between the mill towns of Guilford and Skowhegan. The Trappers' Weekend was held on the fairgrounds located off Route 150 (which is another addition to the Somerset Triangle). MUFON reported a remarkably strange encounter that two men endured one night while camping at the fairgrounds.

The day started early for Randy and Gene (pseudonyms). Trapping was their forte, but as trapper outings go, it was nice for them to interact with their counterparts. As night fell, the men decided to camp out on the fairgrounds, ensuring an early start to the next day's activities. They found a remote area, away from the others, and rested a bit. Around two o'clock in the morning, Randy was enjoying a cigarette when he observed a bright light hovering about sixty feet above a pine tree near their camping area. He woke Gene to get his thoughts on the light. He suggested that it was just someone driving a truck through the field. But as they watched, they knew that didn't seem right. The light got so bright, it bathed the entire field in daylight. Awestruck, they both gazed at the object, amazed at the unusual light that was now about one hundred yards away from them. As the light closed in, the two men noticed a red ball of light come out from underneath the original light. It circled above the treetops, swooped down in front of them, and inexplicably vanished. At this point, the bright light descended and did not make a sound as it did so. They described it as "a mothership and a beam of florescent light that was floating in the air with no engine and no sound." Suddenly, the men observed a "chain-link of colored rings." This occurred in front of their tents, and while they watched the colored rings, morning "just blinked on." I mean this quite literally—it was dark and two o'clock in the morning, and then it was daylight. The bright light and red chain-link lights were gone, and it was approximately four hours later. The two friends were shaken and confused by what they had witnessed, and were utterly in shock that morning had arrived in an instant.

Later, in an effort to determine what had occurred, the men contacted author and investigator Raymond Fowler. After meeting with the men, he advised them to seek the assistance of MUFON to determine what had possibly transpired. In working with the organization, Randy and Gene were introduced to a hypnotherapist to help them bring to light some of the moments of their missing time. The doctor attempted to put Randy under hypnosis, but was unsuccessful. Gene, who was able to be hypnotized, panicked during the session. He was in a highly frightened state and was emotionally and visibly shaken. The doctor took him out of his hypnotic state, and with his teeth chattering, Gene muttered that he could not go on any longer.

The men discarded the idea of learning more and attempted to forget about the encounter and just go about their lives. They tried to find some semblance of normalcy, but it was difficult given the unusual nature of their encounter. Randy suspected that they had been abducted that evening and is currently considering going under hypnosis again. He hopes to learn more about the event. Gene had a very tough go of it for a while and never fully recovered from that fateful night. Although the exact nature of their encounter was never fully understood, it was clearly a life-changing event for both men.

This case was investigated by Valerie Schultz at MUFON and closed as "Unknown."

THE GREAT ESCAPE!

Bangor's classic origins read like those of many other Maine towns described in this book. There's a river running through the city, Native American tribes were already in Penobscot county and settled before Europeans arrived, and there are countless stories involving all aspects of the paranormal. Bangor is also home to probably the most famous of modern writers: me! Just kidding (although I do live in Bangor)—I'm talking about Stephen King! His home, on West Broadway Street, was built in 1858 along with numerous other mansions; the city enjoyed exceptional wealth during this time due to the bustling lumber industry. While some homes have been maintained, others burned during the great Bangor fire of 1911. (The fire started small but quickly spread due to unusually high winds at the end of April that year.) Many of the remaining mansions were converted into apartment houses.

One of these old buildings is where our next encounter begins. According to a report sent to *World UFO Photo and News*, Kyle (pseudonym) was visiting with his brother one evening in October of 2010. After dinner, drinks, and brotherly conversation, Kyle left the apartment at around two o'clock in the morning. As he walked to his vehicle, he heard a female voice call his name. He described it as rhythmic and all-encompassing. He looked around and thought he would find his brother's girlfriend playing a trick on him, but no one appeared to be on the street. The voice continued, and was perceived by Kyle as a "soothing, almost hypnotizing" female voice. His eyes gradually became heavy and his walk slowed to a standstill. Eventually, his eyes closed completely and the voice continued in its tranquil manner: "We're here to help, it's okay, we're not going to harm you, we're going to make you feel better." After a moment, Kyle fainted.

The young man started to wake, his eyes stirring under their lids as he lay motionless. They popped open and instantly ached as a bright light from above blinded him. Kyle's hands reflexively shielded his eyes as he lifted his head to discern his whereabouts. He could see that he was in room that smelled of cleaning solutions and noted that it felt sterile. As he looked around the room he saw two tall, shadowy figures opposite him. The beings frightened him and he looked on in disbelief as they turned to face him. He described what he saw: "Two grey aliens … they had long fingers, very tall, had a little mouth that moved [in an] up and down motion like a fish but nothing was coming out." He clenched his eyes shut, his thoughts manic; he was losing control. He lay there terrified, but had an urge to understand the situation that he was in. He started to control his breathing to calm himself. He wanted to know what was happening to him and tried to speak.

No sound was heard as he mouthed the words he was trying to say. He then realized that his words were interpreted through thought; communications had turned telepathic. They said they did not intend on hurting him. Kyle elaborated: "I asked the aliens if they aren't going to harm me then what are they going to do to me. They replied back, 'we are going to help you and fix you.'" In an instant, the two aliens were on either side of him. They stood him up, and he felt like an escorted prisoner as they walked him to another room. They walked through a corridor, and he could see inside another room to the left and observed more beings: "a huddled circle formation of at least seven to eight greys … "

When they arrived in the second room, he was placed against a board while still in an upright position in the center of the room. He said that this area also smelled of chemicals and that the aliens walked around him, skulking as they looked him over. One of his captors stepped close to him, eye to eye. They stared at each other for a moment, then the entity carefully placed one of its hands over Kyle's nose. He froze with fear as it inserted a black tube into his nostrils. His breathing stopped for a moment, and he gasped and screamed in reaction. He then heard, "It's going to be okay, we are here to help." The voice he had heard previously suddenly came back. It reminded him of an airport's intercom announcement and he could tell it was artificial and trying to calm him. It didn't. They laid him down on the board, and it seemed to hover above the floor. Despite the hypnotic voice continuing, Kyle thrashed about on the table. The aliens struggled to hold him in place, but a leg broke free and he kicked one of his captors! It was with such force that the entity stumbled back, hit the wall, and slid down. The other alien appeared frightened of Kyle and backed away. More entities rushed into the room. The young man looked around and felt overwhelmed and outnumbered. He tried to fight them off as they grabbed him, but he felt weak and dizzy. He fainted once more.

As he came to, he smelt asphalt. He woke up on the side of an unfamiliar road and clumsily stood. He looked around, confused by his surroundings. It was daylight, but he felt that only an hour had passed. He checked his watch and found that it was nearly six o'clock in the morning. He wasn't sure which town he was in and looked for a familiar landmark. Just then, a police officer approached him. He seemed to come out of thin air. Kyle asked him what town he was in and what street he was on. The officer gave him a nasty look and pointed him toward a street sign. From Kyle's perspective, the officer was gone in an instant. He was confused by the officer's hostile demeanor, though he couldn't be sure due to the confused state that he was in.

He was far from his brother's apartment, but he had a friend who lived nearby. When he arrived, he explained the previous night's events. He felt that he was believed, although he knew his friend could see the state that he was in and was trying to be comforting more than anything.

For weeks after his encounter, Kyle was cautious about whom he would share his experience with. His brother and friends did provide him with a support system, but he needed to speak to someone with otherworldly experience. After conducting research on the alien abduction phenomenon, Kyle finally reached out to other Mainers about his experience and spent time at the "Experiencers Speak" conference. These meetings are held annually in southern Maine and are organized by Audrey and Debbie Hewins, founders of Starborn Support, a nonprofit organization that helps alien abduction victims cope with their encounters.

Kyle is still on his journey, and his hope is to find out what truly happened to him and others like him. Despite his first horrid encounter, he has had other experiences that were more pleasant in nature and has found a bit of peace with the aliens. He now feels that they are giving him a message of compassion and love: "Be happy and as loving as possible. This is the message I am getting," he explained.

It is interesting to note that Kyle's perspective is similar to Ed's experience in the story "The Man Who Fell to

Earth," earlier in this book, and to the Travis Walton case from Arizona. Walton has stated in the last few years that he now believes his experience, while traumatic, was to save his life. A theme such as this opens a new paradigm for the abduction experience in popular culture. Films such as *The Fourth Kind* have shown the malevolent nature of alien abductions. We are living in tumultuous times, so perhaps the possibility of compassion, as was perceived by Kyle, Ed, and Travis, is exactly what we need to believe right now.

THE CASE OF
THE SHRUNKEN
BROTHERS

The town of New Gloucester, in Cumberland County in southern Maine, is home to the last active Shaker village in the United States. The Sabbathday Lake Shaker Village is located right off Route 26, about eight miles north of Exit 63 on the Maine Turnpike. An odd encounter happened to two brothers and several of their friends near the village, as reported on the website *UF-Devoe*. While the area is typically serene, this story will make you a bit more vigilant should you find yourself on that road one summer evening.

It was a clear, early summer evening in 1973 when the group was traveling on Route 26. They were actually looking for signs of the infamous "Route 26 Lady in White," who has been reported in the area. They parked near the Shaker Village. Tony (pseudonym) looked out the window from the passenger seat and observed an unusually orange crescent moon in the western part of the sky. He watched the moon for a while and was startled to see it wobble and then descend to a frighteningly low altitude. He brought the oddity to his brother's attention, and they both later recalled the ominous feeling they had when viewing the "moon." They understood that the lighted object was not a celestial body and felt unsafe in the presence of it. As they started to drive again, it kept pace with their car, traveling just above the treetops. Suddenly, the light dipped low in front of the tree line and was close to their vehicle. This frightened the friends, so they turned left and headed toward the town of Oxford to evade the light. As he did so, the environment around them changed. Tony explained, "We noticed that all traffic had ceased on this usually busy and well-traveled road and the sun had gone down awfully fast and now the stars appeared and were HUGE, as if I could reach out to them. We noticed the usual cricket sounds for this area were missing and I could feel and hear my heart beating in my ears as it seemed like we were inside a vacuumed bottle; all we could hear is us talking to each other and all the usual outside noises were silenced." The experience unsettled them, but relief soon set in as the light did not follow their turn off Route 26.

Feeling better, the brothers discussed the light and surmised that it was a genuine UFO since they could not readily identify it. They were anxious to get home to tell their mother of the encounter and as they rounded a bend, an apple orchard came into view. Terror filled them as the light hovered silently over the orchard as if waiting for them. They slammed on the brakes, the light dimmed slightly, and they observed an object behind the light. Tony wrote, "This UFO was big and round and lit up orange and totally quiet and we all just stared at it…" Nobody spoke as they observed the mysterious object. Scott (pseudonym) recalled Tony getting out of the car and then saying "Let's get the hell out of here!" but all Scott could remember was asking, "What happened? What happened?"

Eventually the UFO had vanished, but neither brother realized it immediately. They seemed to have come out of some sort of hypnotic state. They stared at each other for a moment, then started the car. They drove in silence as they thought about the encounter. As they drove, the evening sky seemed to get brighter, like the sun was just beginning to rise. They checked the time and audibly gasped in trepidation. They found that many hours had passed! The time showed it was now morning, but to them it felt like only an hour had passed.

That thought weighed heavily on their minds as they drove. It went unspoken for a moment, and then the realization washed over them like a remembered dream and they exclaimed to each other that they must have been abducted! They were so frightened by the thought that they reported the event to the Auburn police department. The authorities saw that the boys were bruised, battered, and scared, but in no way could the police confirm their abduction story. They took their statements but did not investigate further. The brothers went to the hospital for treatment. (I contacted the Auburn police department about this incident, but my messages were not returned.)

At the hospital, the boys appeared weak and complained of a burning feeling in their lungs. The staff noticed that the whites of their eyes were orange in color and were concerned that the pair might have the beginning stages of jaundice. Initial urine tests ruled out the disease, but another alarming matter was soon discovered. During the examination, Tony's height and weight were checked and the nurse recorded his height as 5 foot 9. When Tony heard this, he proclaimed to the nurse that it was highly inaccurate and explained that he had recently been measured at school and was over 5 foot 10. The nurse could see how distraught this made the boy and recalibrated the scale to check again. She came up with the same result. Tony explained, "I showed the authorities my eighteenth birthday photo taken about two weeks before our abduction and told them to examine my high school medical records for my physical size and please make out the comparison between then and how I am now, and I asked them how many eighteen-year-olds lose an inch overnight?" The nurses could not provide the boy with a satisfactory answer.

Despite being a bit bruised and battered, the boys were in overall good health. The burning sensation in their lungs ceased, and the hospital released them. They wondered what they could possibly tell their mother, and whether she would believe them. She was of course agitated and angry at them for staying out all night without a phone call and rightfully demanded an answer. The brothers tried to explain what had happened, but she would not listen. She continued to scold them, but as she looked them over, she noticed how frightened the boys were. She saw the bruises on their arms and face and their discolored eyes and knew that something had physically happened to them. She said, "What happened? You both have shrunk [and] what is wrong with your eyes?"

Years later, in 2004, Tony disclosed on the *UF-Devoe* website that this was not their first otherworldly experience and that they regularly saw lights in the sky around their home and experienced paranormal activity. Their other encounters and those of their family can be read on the *UF-Devoe* website.

Of note is the fact that the year of their incident correlates with thousands of other sightings in that same time frame. A chronology of worldwide events can be found on the NICAP (National Investigations Committee of Aerial Phenomena) website under the "Chronos" section. Click on the report titled "1973fullrep" and comb through the multiple unusual encounters. More to the point, check out the reports from April 15 in Pennsylvania, and the October 16 report from Lehi, Utah. You'll find similar descriptions of the UFO that these two brothers described. Lastly, there's a report at the top of the "1973" page of two other young men who were abducted in October of that same year. They seem to have been plagued by similar events; perhaps they are connected.

17

ESCAPE TO
WITCH MOUNTAIN

Wilhelm Reich, a psychoanalyst whose career spanned thirty-five tumultuous years, first began his work after he graduated from the University of Vienna in 1922. His early case studies included working alongside Sigmund Freud, but their relationship was so fraught with complications and disagreements that Freud eventually distanced himself from Reich's controversial practices. Reich was perceived as a radical figure among his peers, and even the patients under his care were leery of him.

The Wonderfully Weird World of Wilhelm

Wilhelm Reich's field of study included sexual energy by way of a chemical called "orgone," which he claimed to have discovered. He claimed that experiments with this chemical were to show its healing properties and in the early 1940s started construction on what he called "orgone accumulators." This device would allow a patient to sit inside of it to harness the orgone chemical, which had numerous health benefits including a claim that it cured cancer.

Reich was often ridiculed by his peers, and a silent campaign against him and his work was launched in the mid-1940s. He then bought a home in the small, remote town of Rangeley, Maine, as he wanted to escape the onslaught of lawsuits and defamation. This campaign would eventually see the destruction of his writings and him being jailed; he eventually died in prison from heart failure in 1957.

In 1951, while still in Rangeley, Wilhelm Reich became a bit of a recluse as he continued his experiments with orgone therapy. Often his son Peter would visit and assist with his father's experiments. During those visits, Reich claimed to have discovered a new energy, which he called "Deadly Orgone Radiation." He blamed this as the cause of Rangeley's desertification issues that year. Reich claimed he could harness the power of the orgone energy and help alleviate the drought concern. To do so, he designed a device called a "Cloud Buster." This device was made up of twelve- to fifteen-foot aluminum pipes constructed on a movable table. The pipes were then wired and inserted into water. Reich argued that this device could unlock the orgone energy in the air and bring rain to a large area of the region. He and his son experimented with the Cloud Buster for a couple of years, painstakingly trying to perfect its performance. According to Myron Sharaf in his book *Fury on Earth*, the *Bangor Daily News* reported that local farmers hired Reich to use the Cloud Buster in their blueberry fields to save that season's crop. On July 6, 1953, Reich fired off his device, and it was reported to have rained that very evening. He saved the farmers' blueberry harvest and proved to the community that he had something quite special.

The following year, the eclectic nature of Reich's research progressed into claims of alien activity in the skies above Rangeley. He purported that their crafts sprayed the area with "deadly orgone radiation." He called these crafts "energy alphas" and described them as "shaped like thin cigars with windows," arguing that if these extraterrestrials went untouched, they would spray this energy around the world, eventually destroying the Earth. Reich then wrote his book *Contact with Space*, describing these encounters and their dangerous potential. He vowed to wage a war against the energy alphas, his weapon of choice being the Cloud Buster. In the evenings, he and his son would sky-watch, searching for the crafts. Once spotted, the Reichs would fire off the Cloud Buster at the alien ships and claimed to drain them of the deadly orgone radiation. One evening he professed to have disoriented one of those crafts with the Cloud Buster, causing it to develop an inability to maintain flight. The UFO was then observed to have released what is referred to in ufology as "Angel Hair" throughout most of Rangeley.

In *Contact with Space*, Reich also explained that the UFOs he fired at had traveled to Rangeley through nearby portals. I could not find any witnesses or reports of portals in and around Rangeley; however, I did speak with witnesses in other unrelated sightings from the area. (The next chapter in this book, "The Woman Who Time Forgot," discusses those encounters.) Interestingly, there is a report out of Casco, Maine, about two hours south of Rangeley, where a portal was reported.

The life and work of Wilhelm Reich is vast, intriguing, controversial, and outright weird. My book, of course, is not a biography of Reich but instead takes a look at how his presence in Maine played a part in the history of UFOs in the state. To get more information on Reich's life and work, I recommend his books *Character Analysis*, *The Function of the Orgasm*, and *Contact with Space*. They will satisfy any enthusiast.

Putnam's Portal

Ken Putnam, a retired government maintenance contractor, contacted me via Facebook Messenger to discuss UFO activity in the Casco area. We exchanged numbers, spoke on the phone a few times, and eventually met in August of 2016. Upon arrival at a local eatery, we discussed Reich's work and Putnam's encounters with UFOs. In the town of Casco, there is a small mountain locally called Pine Hill; Putnam lived on this mountain for years and had an interesting story to tell. He started by saying, "My interests in

UFOs began when I was a young boy, but I got serious in 1972 when I was living in Boston. I met a fellow who told me an experience he'd had. He was walking to school with some of his family members one winter morning when they all observed five UFOs slowly flying over the treetops. Out of fear, they buried themselves into the snow. A few minutes later they poked their heads up, and to their surprise, the UFOs were still there when suddenly all took off at a high rate of speed." He added that his fascination kept his interest piqued throughout the years, and in 1976 he moved to Casco and had a house built up on Pine Hill.

One morning while drinking coffee, Ken had an interesting experience. "I heard this roaring noise unlike any I'd heard in my life; come right over the house," he excitedly explained. "The house shook like there was a severe earthquake. When I looked to see what the hell was happening, I saw two fighter jets not fifty feet over my house! They turned so tight and were circling the peak of the mountain." I asked Ken what he thought they were doing flying so low over that area. "I'll tell ya," he said. "They were looking for the UFO." I asked, "Did that happen often?" He looked at me sarcastically and said, "There's a portal on top of that mountain where they go in and out of, and occasionally jet fighters from Brunswick Naval Air Station (BNAS) scramble to search for these UFOs. But they can never find them because the UFOs go into that portal." I asked Ken if he thought it was the same portal that Wilhelm Reich had referred to in his book. He wasn't sure, but further explained, "I don't think the portals are open all the time; they [UFOs] only use them when they need them. I've watched that mountain for years and I can tell you that portal is about two-hundred feet wide. I watched a UFO, as if it came from behind a curtain into that portal area, passed the line of the portal and disappeared on the other side. The UFO was about fifty feet in diameter and just vanished into that portal. Like it was going inside the mountain peak." Fascinated and taking notes, I wrote down "Investigate Pine Hill, overnight."

Ken added, "A year or two later they sent a P-3 Orion over to the mountain, and it went down. The government went nuts over this and conducted a three-month investigation. They shut down the roads up to the mountain, evacuated homes, brought in dogs, and investigators, it was crazy!" I asked Ken why a P-3 Orion would be flying in the area. He explained that it is a surveillance aircraft, and at the time it was one of the most technologically advanced aircraft that the Navy had, typically used for detecting submarines and maritime patrols. So he assumed it was tracking the UFOs.

A quick search on the internet can confirm Ken's story of a downed P-3 Orion in Maine in 1978. A former safety officer from BNAS was given a briefing on the crash and helped with the recovery. He now maintains a Wiki page on the incident and writes, "During climb out, the #1 engine separated from the aircraft (passing up and over the wing). The Navy claims (disputed by Lockheed [manufacturer of the P-3 Orion]) that this was due to a 'whirl mode' event previously seen in several L-188 (the civilian ancestor to the P-3) accidents. This weakened the wing structure causing the piece outboard of that location to fold up and in, thus separating. This piece struck the port horizontal stabilizer, which sheared off. The aircraft, due to aerodynamic force, pitched nose down, then violently nose up with such force that the 3 remaining engines were flung down off the aircraft. Without the weight of engine #3 and #4 to counteract the lift force of the wing, that starboard wing broke off at the wing root. The body of the aircraft (with the inboard port wing section and starboard horizontal and vertical tail sections rolled inverted and impacted the ground, killing everyone."

UFOs were not mentioned anywhere on the page, so I contacted BNAS, now known as Brunswick Executive Airport. The operator said they do not maintain any of the previous records from when BNAS was operational and that I would have better luck contacting the Navy directly. Duh ... So I wrote them an email in late August of 2016. At the time of this writing, I had not heard back. Safe to say, I've probably been added to some sort of watch list (insert awkward laugh).

Ken and I continued to discuss UFOs, the government, and other related topics as we dined. Before we departed, I asked Ken if there was anything else that he would like to say or add. He suggested, "Get down to that mountain and check it out." Good idea, so I did.

Race to Witch Mountain

I traveled to the Casco area in September of 2016 to conduct an overnight investigation of Pine Hill Mountain. I was hoping to catch a glimpse of a light in the sky or, even more fantastic, UFOs flying in and out of "the portal." I brought along with me a full-spectrum camera, an EMF detector, a parabolic microphone, binoculars, and a digital audio recorder. I followed my smartphone's GPS instructions as I "expertly" navigated the dirt road terrain on my way to find Pine Hill. After numerous turnarounds, dead ends, and reception issues, I was finally at the last turn to head up the mountain.

The last road to get to Pine Hill.

Hacker's Hill near Casco, Maine.

As I turned the corner to drive up the steep, narrow dirt road I was stopped dead in my tracks by Private Property signs, a roped-off road, and a sign that read "Smile, you're on camera." I put my vehicle in park and got out. I scanned the trees and ground for any sign of a camera but found none. "Camouflage," I thought. I took some pictures and got back into the car. I sat there for a moment and thought to myself, "How odd, the one area I need to get to in the hopes of seeing and recording reported UFOs coming and going from a portal on the mountain and it's roped off, and there's cameras?!" That's right, dear readers, your hero author was caught right in the middle of a conspiracy fraught with intrigue and quarantined roads. Or more likely, the road was too dangerous to maneuver and the owners or the town did not want anyone up there hurting themselves. But the cameras ... it didn't make sense. No matter, I had a plan B, and that was Hacker's Hill.

Hacker's Hill is also in the town of Casco, located off Quaker Ridge Road. It is a sprawling twenty-seven-acre area that is 750 feet above sea level, which provides a view of the White Mountains, the nearby Lakes Regions, and Pine Hill. I drove up the long, winding road to the top of Hacker's Hill and parked my vehicle between the trees and cell towers (there are two a stone's throw away). It was about 6:00 p.m. by the time I got there, so I settled in, unpacked my homemade dinner, and waited. I had a full view of all the mountain peaks in the area and my head was "on a swivel."

A few hours passed, during which I finished my meal, sipped on coffee, and went through the various equipment I had with me. Darkness arrived, yet I was vigilant in my pursuit of the portal. I tracked satellites and airplanes. In the distance below, as lights turned on in neighborhood homes, they appeared to me as lazily laid Christmas lights switching on throughout the mountainous area. One light appeared much brighter than the others; it lay just west of Pine Hill. I grabbed my binoculars for a better look. The bright light burned intensely and caused a glare through the binocular's lenses, so I had to look away. "Was this a landed UFO?!" I thought. With the naked eye, it was brighter than the rest of the lights, so again I peered through the binoculars. Once my eyes adjusted I could see an object behind the light: a barn. Looked as though the landed UFO was nothing more than a large bulb atop the roof of an old barn, dang it!

As time ticked away and boredom settled in, I looked at the time—1:03 a.m. I forged ahead and continued my pursuits with more sips of my coffee, cigarettes, and a full scan of the sky every couple of minutes; sometimes inside the car, sometimes outside of it. Of note is that while outside my car, I heard an odd sound from some type of "animal" coming from the tall grass in front of me. I had never heard a sound like that before, and I can only describe it as some sort of weird groan as it stalked through the grass. It was getting closer, and I don't play, y'all, so I got back into my car and turned on the headlights. If you can believe it, my eyes were clenched shut, and as I slowly opened them, my mind envisioned all the ghastly figures that might appear before me: Sasquatch, Dogman, Jason Voorhees!

With my lids fully open, the scene wasn't as horrific as I had expected. In reality, there was nothing. Just the tall grass blowing in the wind. The animal was probably harmless, and it seemed my imagination was getting the better of me. At this point I decided to try some UFO summoning. This is not the sort of activity I am typically interested in trying, but as the hours ticked by and there was no sign of UFOs, I thought "What the hell" and gave it a go. Before my trip, I'd researched some techniques by way of James Gilliland. You can research more about "Gilliland Ranch" at his *ECETI* website. The ranch is a paranormal hotspot with reports of UFOs, Sasquatch, and more, located in south-central Washington State within the Mount Adams wilderness area.

I started my mental summoning by repeating, "Please reveal yourselves to me." I laughed to myself and thought "What the hell am I doing?" I felt awkward yet open to the idea, much like documentarian Mitch Fillion must have felt in his film *Calling Occupants,* in which he and some friends attempt UFO summoning with startling results. I thought "If Mitch can do it, so can I!" I raised my fist triumphantly and smirked. (If you would like to check out Mitch's documentary, it can be viewed on his *Near Death Films* website.)

About ten minutes passed and nothing happened. With my head still on a swivel, I looked behind me for the umpteenth time, out over the water. To my surprise, a light was just sitting there! It hovered above the water, silent and motionless. It hadn't been there before, and I fumbled for my cameras. I used my cell phone and the full-spectrum cam and started recording. As I did this, a vehicle drove into the parking area, less than one hundred yards from me. Concerned, I stopped recording until I figured out it was a car full of college-aged fellas enjoying some "recreational use," if you know what I mean. I turned back around to continue recording the light and was frustrated to see that it was gone. I scanned the entire skyline to no avail, though I did have about nineteen seconds of it recorded on my phone. It can be viewed on my YouTube channel (search

"Nomar Slevik") or by typing the title "Hacker's Hill UFO" into the YouTube search bar.

I stayed up on the hill for another couple of hours and eventually decided it was time to make the trek back to my hotel. The next morning, I surveyed my footage again. Although interesting, the video showed nothing more than a light in the sky. Nonetheless, I was glad I had captured it and wondered if my "summoning" had actually worked. Who knows? I then listened to my audio recorder that had been running the entire night, just in case. Unfortunately, most of it was either whatever music I was playing, the wind, or plain silence. I was starting to feel a little discouraged about it all when I said to myself, "No, that is not fair. You came to the mountain and recorded a friggin' light in the sky and that's cool as hell. You should feel good about this."

I agreed with my inner thoughts and prepared to write this story. I referred to my notes and audio recording from my meeting with Ken. I researched some more information about the area and rewatched the video from my cell phone. I began feeling a sense of pride in the effort I had put forth and felt good about the potential this story had. I hope you agree with me, and that it sparks you to do some research of your own. Check out the video I shot and the pics from the mountain. And if nothing else, you can tell your friends about Nomar, the investigator who was thwarted in his attempts to report on the portal… Or you could just tell them about Reich, the orgone-crazed UFO fighter from Rangeley.

THE WOMAN WHO TIME FORGOT

The blizzard of 2017 dumped more than three feet of snow in parts of Maine between February 12 and 13. While it is safe to say that most Mainers got through the storm just fine, it was a surprise to many how much snow we got in such a short amount of time. During the height of the storm, the blowing snow created near whiteout conditions and visibility was so poor that the Maine Department of Transportation had to halt plowing operations in the Mid-Coast, Down East, and Bangor areas. That's bad. I was there, shoveling it out of my driveway in Bangor. My girlfriend and I spent a total of five hours manually removing the hellish white punishment. It got to a point where we had no place to put it, as the banks in our driveway were already above our waists! We ended up having to haul the snow out to the street and let the city plows get rid of it for us.

Fast-forward a few days, to reports that a new storm was headed our way for midweek that could bring us an additional twelve inches of snow! Thankfully it did not hit as hard as meteorologists had originally thought, and we came away unscathed with a mere two to three more inches of the white stuff.

February 12 held another point of significance for me: I was looking forward to meeting Sue, a UFO witness from Stratton, but the storm forced us to cancel our meeting. We rescheduled for the following Sunday, February 19. I had first heard of Sue's story from an issue of the *Portland Phoenix* from February 2012; oddly enough, this was almost four years to the day from when the article was published. Synchronistic, yeah?

My colleague Erik Cooley and I met Sue for coffee at an inn located in Stratton. The two-hour drive from Bangor led us through the aftermath of the blizzard, allowing us a glimpse at the snowfall that had been survived by folks in Palmyra, Skowhegan, Anson, Kingfield, Rangeley, Stratton, and all the other small towns we drove through. The snowbanks in these areas easily surpassed Bangor's, and the people from there reminded me of people I knew when my family lived in Fort Kent. No matter how remote they were or how much weather they got, they survived and smiled through it. Just like the smile Sue gave us upon our arrival at the restaurant.

A petite, older woman, Sue greeted us warmly and asked how our drive had been. She was a spunky, friendly woman. We exchanged pleasantries and quickly got to the reason for our meeting. She told us, "When this whole thing started, '91–'92, I would have the weirdest dreams, and this Pink Floyd song would be playing in the background. After so many years of this, I got into the band because I had to know what song it was. Turns out it was 'Interstellar Overdrive' and you know what, it was the strangest thing this morning. I got in the car to drive over here to meet you, and that damn song was playing when I turned on the radio!" The synchronicity was not lost on her, and we were riveted.

Psychoanalyst Carl Jung developed the synchronicity concept, which holds that some events in one's life tend to be "meaningful coincidences." In an interview I'd had with Skowhegan psychic Shalel Way, I'd learned about synchronicities. Shalel discussed the impact of it on one's life, and even had a synchronistic moment with me that involved my birth date as it related to a UFO sighting she'd had in the '70s.

Sue went on to say that dreams played a sincerely odd role in her life. "I've never dreamed as myself except for those Pink Floyd dreams." I asked her what she meant and she said that her interest in dreams started with a car accident. "When I was fifteen I got my license. You know the bridge in Anson? It's a newer bridge and they got it because of me. I went off that bridge, forty-two feet down to the water in my father's station wagon. We should have never lived through it. I'd picked up two people and we were headed to the dance. The way the car landed, there was a seven-foot wall on each side, and I landed right in the middle of it with two inches to spare each side. They said two inches this way, or two inches that way, would have broken the car right in half. We walked away from it."

After being released from the hospital that same night, she got home and learned about a woman named Ruth Montgomery from the nightly news. Montgomery had just published a book called *Strangers Among Us*, in which she explored the "walk-in" concept. Montgomery wrote that walk-ins "are high-minded entities permitted to take over the bodies of human beings who wish to depart this life."

This concept fascinated Sue, and after surviving such an event, it made her pause and analyze her dreams. She thought that she may be dreaming someone else's memories. She explained, "After that car accident, I can't remember some things from my past. Even to this day, I have trouble remembering aspects of my past. It seemed really strange that some of the memories that I do have belong to someone else." She wondered if she might be a walk-in.

The strangeness continued with a UFO sighting in 1991. While living in Clinton, Sue and her then-husband were getting ready to lie in bed and watch a movie. Her kids were downstairs just about to watch a movie of their own. It was a little before 9:00 p.m. when Sue noticed a light outside her bedroom window. "It was bright! Beaming bright! Right above the tree line," she said. "I watched it for about five minutes and then showed it to my husband." Sue's husband expressed confusion about the odd light and both decided to go outside for a better look. As they walked through the living room, the kids inquired why they were going outside. "I told them there was a weird light, and sure enough they filed in line behind us." Each family member stepped outside slowly, watching the light as they moved. Gathered together on the porch, they stood in silence, unsure of what they were witnessing.

Unexpectedly, the light instantly ascended. Audible gasps were heard from the family. "What is that, mom?" asked the older of the two children. "They weren't scared, they just didn't know what it was," she explained. None of them did. So they continued to watch as it hovered at the higher altitude. Again, without warning, the light moved and hovered directly in front of their home. This time it was closer and lower, as if it were watching them. She said, "You didn't see it move. It was just there. It was so weird. We didn't see it move!"

I anxiously sipped my coffee and asked, "What time do you think you went outside?" Sue again explained that they went outside just before 9:00 p.m. and that the entire sighting lasted about five or six minutes, and then it vanished.

"It was just gone. It blinked out, so we went in the house. We walked through the door and the kids exclaimed that the movie was over." I looked at Sue, confused. "I know, I told the kids, no, it's just beginning. They said no it's not, it's over, what time is it?" Sue went to check the time and found that it was almost 11:00 p.m. "We didn't really discuss it. Everyone was aware of it. I didn't want to discuss it, my husband didn't. So, no one did."

No other oddities were reported that night or in the coming weeks. The missing time was weird enough, but then the dreams started.

It was after her sighting in 1991 that Sue began experiencing the odd dreams with the Pink Floyd song. In the dream, "all of a sudden, we're on a spaceship and everything is white. We're on this damn spaceship, my husband and I, and everything is white!" I asked her what she meant by "everything is white." She said, "Everything, I mean everything. The walls, our clothes. It was weird. And then every time my husband would open his mouth to talk, the Pink Floyd song would play." Erik and I shared a confused look. She continued, "We then made our way to an elevator. There were windows everywhere, too. When we got out of the elevator, the doors opened to something like a Walmart. It was clothes and they were all white! Everything was either my size or my husband's size and white! And that damn song kept playing, it was blasting. I had that dream for years."

Enthralled, Erik asked, "Anyone else in the dream other than you and your husband?" "Nope, just me and him," she said. "And that song playing every time he would try to talk. Big windows everywhere, and we could see the stars." Erik added, "Anyone else have weird dreams?" Sue did not recall anyone else mention odd dreams.

Sarah (pseudonym), the owner of the inn, walked in during this point in our conversation and looked the three of us over. "We're discussing the lights," Sue said to her. She smiled and shook our hands. Sue gestured to me and said, "Yeah, he's writing a book about UFOs and such."

The *Portland Phoenix* reported an encounter that Sarah and some of her patrons had had on Christmas Eve a few years back: "One Christmas Eve, one guy goes out to smoke a cigarette, and he says to me, come on out here and look at this light." Sarah and others joined the gentleman, and all observed a bright light in the sky. She explained that it would dart left to right, and after a little while it would move elsewhere. Sarah and the bunch watched the light for over an hour.

Then a waitress stopped by the table and said, "You guys heard what Jeff saw, right? On 16." She looked at Sarah and Sue for recognition and received it. Jeff (pseudonym), a friend of Sue and Sarah's, was traveling home on Route 16 one evening in 2005 and witnessed a bell-shaped object in the sky. The *Portland Phoenix* quoted his description: "It was four stories high and floating by somebody's house."

This sighting recalled the Kecksburg case out of Pennsylvania in 1965. In that incident, an object was observed screeching through the sky like a meteor, but it began making turns and slowing down. Eventually it hit the ground in the woods of Kecksburg. Area residents who saw the object had likewise described it as bell-shaped. But it was not nearly as big as the object Jeff witnessed.

You can watch a documentary about the Kecksburg UFO right now on YouTube by searching for "Kecksburg UFO Incident." Also, the documentary production company Small Town Monsters produced a film entitled *Invasion on Chestnut Ridge*, directed by Seth Breedlove.

About ten years before Jeff's sighting, Sue had had another strange incident. It was 1995; she was recently divorced and moved to Cape Cod. She developed some back pain and was concerned, so on a friend's recommendation, Sue paid a visit to a doctor who ran a chiropractic business in Orleans, Massachusetts, and he took her on as a patient. Sue said weakly, "I'm starting to shake, because this is where it gets weird. My doctor said that he needed to take some X-rays." Once the X-rays came back, the doctor called Sue and asked her to come in. She explained how their conversation went: "I walked in and he says, 'When were you shot?'" "What?!" answered Sue. "Seriously though, when were you abducted by aliens?" Sue's face went serious, but she laughed it off and asked, "What are you talking about?" The doctor motioned for her to come look at the X-rays.

The one he had showing was of her left hip. He pointed to an area and asked, "What the hell are those?" Sue explained that the X-ray showed three metal spheres in the shape of a triangle, and he'd written on it, "Unknown Metal Objects in Pelvic Area." "A shotgun bullet would not do that," she said excitedly. "Besides, I've never been shot. There's no marks there. No scars or anything!" Sue and the doctor discussed the strangeness of the objects, though he did not recommend their removal as they were not harming her in any way. Sue provided me with her doctor's name. I called his practice in Massachusetts to get his take on this anomaly, but my messages went unanswered.

Months later, Sue met a gentleman by the name of Rod C. Davis. He is a paranormal researcher and author who spent time in the Stratton area as a youth and young adult. They discussed Sue's metal spheres, and he recommended that she have them surgically removed and get them tested to see what they were. Sue declined this option, as she did not want to have surgery. However, she did give it some consideration.

A little more than a year later, Sue came down with pneumonia. She contacted her doctors and during her visit, they advised that X-rays were needed. She boldly asked them to also take an X-ray of her hip. Her doctor was confused, but Sue insisted and, surprisingly, her doctor obliged. After seeing the new X-ray of her hip, she called Rod Davis. Before she could get the words out he said, "They're gone, aren't they?" "How did you know that?" she asked. Rod explained that the mere mention of the metal spheres brings attention to them, and "they" do not like that. He added, "You were being tracked, you talked about them too much." Sue then called her chiropractor from Orleans and exclaimed, "They're gone!" He was confused and asked Sue what she meant. "The metal balls are gone!" She said that her doctor couldn't believe it and went to check his files and found that Sue's original X-rays were now inexplicably missing. This confused him, as he kept meticulous records.

Our waitress at the restaurant handed Sue her order of toast. In between bites, she told us of another story that happened a little while later, after she moved to the Stratton area from Massachusetts with her boyfriend. "We decided one day to go up to Kennebago. My boyfriend makes furniture out of moose antlers and we went up to the woods to look for some." They arrived at a clearing near the woods at 8:00 a.m. After a brief discussion, her boyfriend was to take one route, and Sue and her dog another, and they would meet in an hour. After walking for a while, she found that she was lost. She did have a walkie-talkie with her, so she turned it on to radio her boyfriend. "I knew I was lost. Kennebago Mountain is a big area. I was walking and walking but I was lost. We just put fresh batteries in the walkie-talkies so I turned it on to admit to him that I was lost." We shared a smile at her comment. She continued, "All of a sudden this screech came on and then nothing. It was dead!

You gotta be kidding me, I don't know where in the hell I am, and I've got no battery? So, I walked."

Eventually, Sue found Saddleback Mountain and knew she had to walk in the opposite direction. Finally, after about an hour and a half, she heard a vehicle honking. As she approached the direction of the noise, she saw her boyfriend's truck; he was honking to help her find her way. "He knew I was lost. But he was not happy. He asked where I had been. I told him I got lost and I tried the walkies but the battery died." The boyfriend looked at her, confused. "Sue," he says to me, "you know how long you've been gone? You've been gone for four hours. It's noon!" Sue couldn't believe it. She thought she had only been gone for about an hour and a half. I asked her if she had any odd moments that she could not explain while on her walk, but she said no. It was just her and her dog trying to find their way. Nothing seemed out of the ordinary other than being lost. "I lost that time. And the walkies, it didn't make sense to us."

She has not had any other experiences that she can remember. "I still wonder," she said, and I asked her if she had or would be interested in utilizing hypnotic regression. She said she would be interested so I did put her in contact with a source, though no sessions have been completed yet.

As the stories unfolded before us, Erik and I couldn't help but ask ourselves if there was something about the area that attracted all the strangeness. Could it be the nondescript military presence (the Navy has a SERE school in the region), or perhaps imaginations have a knack of running a bit wild here. Sue said, "The more you dig into the questions of this area, the more questions you find." Regardless of one's opinion of the area and the stories told, the perception of the population is one of high strangeness. We also discussed how the people in this area might be more attuned to their surroundings because there are not as many distractions in their rural environment, and this could lend itself to odd sights and sounds being more easily observed.

As Erik and I were wrapping up our conversation, Sue looked at us with lost, honest eyes and made a somber inquiry. She asked, "I've got nothing to gain by it. I just want to know, why me?" We looked at each other, wishing that we had an answer or some sort of explanation, but we didn't.

THE TIME DAD SAW A SPACECRAFT

In the thick of Down East Maine, nestled within the Passamaquoddy reservation and Forest City, you'll find the town of Steuben. Considered a fishing village and located just east of Gouldsboro, it was first settled in 1760 and eventually incorporated in February of 1795. The town gets its name from a German soldier named Baron Wilhelm von Steuben, who is credited with working alongside the United States during the Revolutionary War. Nowadays, folks in the area live like most Mainers, hardworking and enjoying their families.

Once you get through the center of town, just a little way from the library and grammar school, the area turns rural. There are homes, filled with families, that crowd each side of the roadway. One such family was settled in for the evening after having finished work and school. With their routines in place, supper finished, and homework done, they never could have imagined the sight they were about to witness in a few short hours. It never occurs to anyone. It just happens, and life becomes a little different. I found the kernel of this story on the *Phantoms & Monsters* site and the *Wakonda 666* blog.

Zachary (pseudonym) was a quiet boy. He had friends but enjoyed keeping to himself. He played sports and went on overnight stays at his friend's house. What truly made him happy, though, was reading, watching movies, and hanging with his dad. One night he had fallen asleep in front of the television, just like he'd done only a million times or so, when he was awoken by his father and stepmother hollering from outside, "Zack!! Get out here!! You have to come see this!!" Zack got up, stumbling a bit due to the deep sleep he had been in, and hurriedly made his way outside. "What are you guys doing?" he said and noticed that his father was holding a camera and looking up into the sky. His father responded, "There was a ... well, I don't know. What would you say, hon? A spacecraft?" His stepmother just looked at her husband, mouth agape, and then looked at Zack, gesturing with her hands and shaking her head as if to say "I don't know."

Zack couldn't believe what his father was saying. His dad was never one to make up stories or show any interest in UFOs. He was a get up before dawn, have some coffee, get to work, come home, watch the news, and go to bed type of guy. But there he was, on the porch in the middle of the night, excited about UFOs. Zack smiled, walked closer, and asked, "What did it look like?" His father was searching for the right words and said, "Zack, it was a large craft just hovering, no noise. It had blue lights on top and these pulsating, white lights going around the bottom." Zack's eyes got big. He just couldn't believe it. "And guess what, Zacky? I got a picture of it."

Zack was utterly dumbfounded. There he was, standing on the porch with his father who previously had no interest in UFOs, yet he had a picture of one!? Zack immediately asked to see the photo. In the chaos of it all, his father hadn't thought to look at it yet. The glow of the digital camera's screen bathed the excited expressions on their faces in a warm blue hue. His father eagerly fumbled with the camera's buttons when it finally appeared on screen. Most of the image was shrouded in darkness, but in the center of the photo some lights could be seen; Dad zoomed in. A blue outline in the shape of an elongated oval was observed. Below it ran a gamut of white lights. The trio on the porch, in the middle of the night, were flabbergasted. The father said that the picture did the craft no justice, but he was happy that there was evidence of what he had seen. Zack was speechless and could only stare at the image. They stayed outside for quite some time afterwards, but nothing else was observed.

Once inside and settled, Zack uploaded the image to his computer and wrote down the chain of events. He asked his father what brought the light to his attention. "It was kinda weird, actually," his father started. "I felt the need to go outside; when I did it was right there, like it was waiting for me. I looked at it for a minute or so and then called for you guys to come out. She was out first, so I ran in to get the camera, took a shot, and hollered for you again. That about sums it up." This seemed agreeable to Zack, and he continued his documentation. The pair eventually reported their sighting and made the picture publicly available. You can view the photo on Lon Strickler's website or by doing a Google image search for "Steuben Maine UFO."

For weeks after the sighting, Zack's father sky-watched almost every evening in hopes of catching another glimpse of the "spacecraft." Some nights, Zack was out there with him, but other times he was in his room reading or watching a movie. Inevitably, he'd pull out the photo and look out at the sky from his bedroom window, hoping for a glimpse as well. He'd stare at the stars in sincere wonder. There was a sense of comfort he felt because he knew something that others did not. He knew that life beyond Earth was real.

STRANGERS BY THE LAKE

The year 1968 was a historical one, full of emotional and political triumphs and tragedies. An abundance of vastly dynamic events occurred. These included the assassinations of Martin Luther King Jr. and Robert F. Kennedy, a stance against racism that was felt during the Olympics when African American medal winners took their honors with a bowed head and a raised fist, and the launch of the Tet Offensive in Vietnam, which could be considered the catalyst for the eventual withdrawal of the United States' involvement in the war. Also, the Apollo 8 rocket was launched, which became the first human-habited orbit of the moon, and of course Richard Nixon was elected our country's thirty-seventh president (inaugurated in '69). Many a Mainer was wrapped up in the war and the election;

Hubert Humphrey won over 55 percent of Maine's vote. It seemed like the state was filled with both war supporters and detractors, and the economy was in question due to closing military bases.

While the first known use of the term "vacationland" for Maine occurred in 1927, it was during the early 1960s that Maine adopted the term for its slogan. While the idea seemed far from Mainers' minds as Nixon took office and war support soured, a trip to a "vacationland" is what a lot of people around the nation felt they needed during tumultuous times. In the summer of '68, the state had a resurgence of tourism due to so many people feeling the effects of the current culture in America.

"Vacationland" is indeed an appropriate term for the state's vast coastline, lakes, and gorgeous villages. Sebago Lake is most certainly one of those areas, coveted and well-visited by out-of-towners and locals alike. Located in Cumberland County, the lake borders multiple towns, including Windham, which served as the location for a most peculiar encounter. The origins of the following story come from the website *UFO Hunters*.

Andrew (pseudonym) was about ten years old in 1968, and as a treat his father took him and his younger brother to Sebago Lake on an overnight camping trip. They planned for a day of fishing and fun on the water, and a whimsical night of sleeping in a tent. That night was the first time Andrew and his brother were allowed to sleep in their own tent, although Dad was nearby in his. After they cooked up the day's catch, roasted some marshmallows, and told ghost stories, all three settled in for the night.

Hours later, Andrew awoke sleepy-eyed, and a bathroom stop was needed. He cautiously unzipped the tent flap so as to not wake his brother and stepped out into a brightly moonlit landscape. He found an area not far from the camp to do his business, but heard some commotion coming from the water's edge. This caused him to duck behind a nearby bush and watch as shadowy figures spoke in a language he did not understand. As Andrew recalled, "While crouched, I heard voices … " He noticed that the figures had big, black, piercing eyes and were naked!

The young boy was confused and frightened by what he saw, and he stood to run away. Just as he did this, the beings approached him and concentrated their stare on him. Andrew felt like they were reading his mind and body. He froze, scared that he might be kidnapped by crazed, naked creepers. However, as they got closer, he could see that he had been mistaken about their lack of clothing— all three were wearing skintight suits or uniforms. Two of the figures were short in stature, and the third was much taller; to Andrew, the latter seemed to be the one in charge. Even though he was frightened, he wanted to know what the beings were doing at the campsite.

The taller of the three approached the boy, who spoke telepathically to him. Using this form of communication surprised Andrew; he remarked, "I felt as though he talked to my brain and my brain answered! My mouth did not move, I put my hands on my lips, I felt them not move."

The tall being continued his telepathic connection and explained that their presence was merely to learn about the boy. Andrew considered this for a moment, but then looked at the two other figures. He described them as having terrifying faces, and he could sense that they wanted to harm him in some way. He did not believe the taller being's reasoning. More than once, he tried to run away but found that he could not move. One of the shorter figures continued to stare menacingly at him. Andrew described his thoughts during that time as follows: He "wanted to do awful things to me ... his face was more scrunched and wrinkled with a brownish pink naked skin. Long arms, not hairy, just weak-looking arms with long fingers."

The "ugly" being then spoke, audibly, in a high-pitched voice that Andrew described as "squiggled." He could not understand its language but felt negative intent. The taller being tried again to reassure Andrew, but the boy felt distrustful of the situation and asked the taller being what they could possibly learn from a child. As he recounts, "I could only as a child think, what on Earth do you want with a kid? Aren't you here to teach the big people how to behave? We have a war going on."

Andrew was referring to the Vietnam War, which caused him a lot of stress as a child. Years later, he thought about this moment and questioned ever having had the encounter in the first place. He wondered if the event could be a kind of PTSD effect, asking whether his story could be some sort of rationalization he'd created in his life or "memories [that] are just a result of trauma of the Vietnam war? … You will never know how many times I have asked myself. If it is just a bad dream, why do I have that burnt-in-my-brain feeling there?"

After the taller being spoke again, Andrew remembered his brother alone in the tent and suddenly became deathly scared for his brother's safety. After he had that realization, he was able to break out of whatever hypnotic state he was in, and he ran back to the tent. He huddled by his brother's side and could hear the beings approach. He hid under the covers and kept repeating in his head, "If I can't see you, you can't see me." Miraculously, their presence faded. He could no longer hear them outside, and peeked to be sure.

Morning arrived quickly, causing Andrew to think that time had sped forward. Or, and perhaps more terrifying, missing time may have occurred. If so, he wanted to know what it meant. He asked himself, "Did they take me somewhere?" He had a sense that his brother was taken as well, and despite having no memory of being abducted, his impression was that it most likely happened. Throughout the years, he remembered more visitations with the strange beings. He cannot recall any actual abduction scenarios, only telepathic conversations, but fears that his abduction memories may have been blocked.

After Andrew's daughter was born, the beings visited him once again. Although his memories of the encounter are sparse, he does recall that the conversation involved his daughter. This made him angry, and he refused to let her be involved with them. He felt as though he took a stand against them during that conversation and like his voice was finally heard. He has not been visited since.

Despite his admission that the encounters could be a byproduct of post-traumatic stress disorder (PTSD), Andrew still had an unsettled feeling about the encounters. The events felt real to him, and he was convinced that more happened during the "conversations" than what he remembered. Regardless, he was thankful that the visitations had ceased.

Post abduction syndrome (PAS) is a theory that holds that people who have experienced one or more alien abductions (especially as children) could develop anxiety-induced stress, similar to PTSD. My thought is that Andrew could suffer from PAS, or a hybrid of PAS and PTSD. The syndrome was studied in 1992 by Dr. David M. Jacobs, Budd Hopkins, and Dr. Ron Westrum in their report *Unusual Personal Experiences: An Analysis of the Data from Three Major Surveys*. Registered nurse Rose Hargrove wrote a dissertation on PAS called "Post Abduction Syndrome (PAS): Description of an Emerging Syndrome," which gained notoriety in 2000. The medical professionals involved with these studies had combined experiences in Advanced Cardiac Life Support (ACLS), the operating room, the emergency room, intensive care, PTSD, psychology, psychiatry, and more. Furthermore, Hargrove was a field investigator and abduction consultant for MUFON.

Perhaps Andrew's mental state from having been in combat, coupled with multiple alien encounters from childhood, created a hybrid anxiety syndrome that's yet to be diagnosed. I did conduct a phone interview about my thoughts on the matter, but was advised that without meeting with the witness in person, it would be impossible to diagnose him. Fair enough. But I would argue that this hybrid syndrome, should it exist *and* go untreated, could complicate one's mental wellbeing further.

Andrew seems to have adjusted well since the encounters stopped. Reflecting on the impact, he wrote, "I believe I have in some odd way gotten used to them … if there was something to be done to me or others they only needed to ask!" How dignified.

THE TALE OF TWO BROTHERS AND A TR-3B

The town of Strong, Maine, was first a part of Township Number Three, First Range North of Plymouth Claim, West of Kennebec River (or T3 R1 NPC WKR). Whew! Later it was renamed Readstown, since it was settled by William Read in 1784; seventeen years after that, it would be purchased and incorporated by the State of Massachusetts and named after their governor, Caleb Strong. This small Maine town was once heralded as the pinnacle of politics and craftsmanship due to claims that the Republican Party was first born here, *and* that it was once home to the Strong Wood Products Company, which in its heyday was manufacturing over twenty million toothpicks a day!

The Sandy River enters Strong from the west, through a valley near the mountains, and runs through other towns in the surrounding area. Strong's lengthy agricultural and fishing history continues to this day, with many residents taking advantage of the pristine land and water that they call home. The Sandy River plays a big role in the lives of fishermen in the area, a couple of whom had their own unique story to tell. Culled from the MUFON database, the following story is yet another addition to the town's fantastic history.

Summer in Strong brings many people to the river for daylong activities, and back in 1978, folks were no different. Two brothers enjoyed these activities, especially eel fishing, which could bring them some extra spending money when they sold eel as bait to striper fisherman. Eel fishing with nets is usually done at night as eels move downriver during the summer season, making them easier to catch. One late-July night, these two brothers were out in the Sandy River netting a big haul of eel. They were excited to sell them the next day for a big chunk of cash. As they packed up for the night, they heard a strange sound from somewhere above, and both looked up to see what could be the source of the noise. One of the brothers shared that they "heard a whooshing sound, like the wind, directly overhead." When they looked up, they were startled to see a large black triangle with lights at each point slowly flying across the sky. It flew silently, seemingly oblivious to any observer below. The boys were frightened but could not look away, and feared that it was flying too slowly to be a conventional aircraft. The other brother explained the object's features and speed: "Each point had a fixed colored light (not blinking), red, blue, and green. The round lights were at least ten feet in diameter, much bigger than any man-made aircraft lights I've seen otherwise. The triangle was an estimated three hundred feet each side. The craft was approximately three hundred to four hundred feet above us and made no noise except the sound of the craft cutting the air. The speed of the craft was about twenty miles per hour, too slow to be a conventional aircraft."

They were able to watch the craft for some time as it flew slowly out of sight. One brother thought it was an experimental military aircraft, and he might not be wrong. Black triangle UFOs (now typically called TR-3Bs) have risen exponentially since the 1970s with an intriguing wave of them in Belgium from 1989 to 1990. A photo can be viewed in the book *UFOs Caught on Film* (page 64), or by doing a Google Image search for "Belgium UFO." In June of 2016, an impressive Black Triangle video was released and subsequently reported by the UK website *Express*, and also submitted to MUFON. The video can be viewed on YouTube by searching for "UK TR3B." If you watch the video, you'll find that it strikes an eerily similar note to the brothers' sighting in Maine.

Black triangle UFOs have been the subject of much scrutiny, especially since the story of Randy Cramer became known. This phantasmagorical story claims that Randy spent twenty years in outer space, training as a soldier on Mars and fighting a war with aliens. He states that during this time, he was transported from Earth to Mars in a government made TR-3B Black Triangle spacecraft. Some believe that the TR-3B is part of a secret government program called "Aurora," described by the website *Dark Government* as follows: "triangular-shaped, nuclear powered aerospace platform was developed under the Top Secret, Aurora Program with SDI and black budget monies. The Aurora is the most classified aerospace development program in existence. The TR-3B is the most exotic vehicle created by the Aurora Program. It is funded and operationally tasked by the National Reconnaissance Office, the NSA, and the CIA."

Interesting, to say the least. I do implore you to research the Randy Cramer case. You can start by visiting his website, *Earth Citizen Consulting.*

As for those two brothers who were eel fishing on a warm July night in 1978, well, they weren't sure what to make of the craft and watched it as it flew out of sight. Over thirty years later, they finally reported their sighting to MUFON. To this day, they still look up, and one brother claimed to have had at least nine other encounters with otherworldly craft. Shalel Way, the psychic from Skowhegan, also has observed UFOs over the Sandy River and said, "There were two of them hovering over cars by the Sandy River in '84." (More on Shalel a few pages from now.)

To me, the brothers' tale appears to be candid and genuine. I believe they saw something that night. To call it an alien spacecraft, or even a government-funded aerospace platform with the capabilities to fly out of our atmosphere *and* to other planets ... I am not ready to do that just yet.

THE DARK SKIES OF ORRINGTON

By Erik Cooley and Nomar Slevik

Just beyond the city lights of Bangor and Brewer lies the small town of Orrington. Originally a part of Kenduskeag plantation, Orrington branched out on its own to become an officially established town in 1812. Coincidentally, this was the same year as the war that led to Maine eventually gaining its independence from Massachusetts.

Although not as full of the glitz and glamour of "city" life as its two neighbors, Orrington serves as a connector to the bigger cities of the north and its fellow towns along the Penobscot River when heading south. Route 15 is the major byway through the town and leads to several different concentrated developments that make up the town. But as you will soon read, Route 15 is not just a roadway through the town of Orrington—as reported by Michelle Souliere's blog *Strange Maine,* it's a thruway to the unknown.

One midsummer night in June of 2015, a witness reported that when leaving the local gas station at Snows Corner, headed north on Route 15, he encountered a bright, teal-colored object in the sky. The object reportedly dipped up and down behind the tree line, was triangular in shape, and had a rounded bottom. Although the encounter didn't last long, the witness estimated less than a minute, it left an impression with him. Eventually the craft flew out of sight below the tree line, never to be seen again. Struck by the curiosity one would naturally have after encountering such an unexplainable occurrence, the witness immediately pulled his truck over in the hopes of sighting the object again. He drove to the next road over but saw nothing. Still in shock and surprised by the encounter, the witness drove home, grabbed binoculars, and attempted to find the UFO. He felt the binoculars would provide the sight needed to locate the mysterious object, and so headed to the town line of Orrington-Brewer.

Upon arrival near the UFO's last sighting, the witness parked his truck and walked the railroad tracks. He looked up and searched for some time, but the object did not appear. He felt defeated; he truly wanted to understand what this mysterious object was and pondered plausible explanations for the occurrence in his head. "Was it a drone?" he thought. There was no indication of anyone nearby who could have operated it. Also, the lights didn't appear similar to lights on any man-made craft he'd seen previously. The witness recalled thinking the color of the craft was almost as bizarre as the behavior itself!

Of note, there are other documented incidents in Orrington. One appeared in a *Bangor Daily News* article in June of 1978 titled "Object in Sky Upsets Orrington Woman." The previously mentioned Route 15 is the site of this peculiar encounter as well. The witness was driving through the Wheelers Hill area when suddenly she felt like she had been jolted by a pulse of electricity. She reported seeing an enormous red ball of light that seemed to emit a tremendous amount of heat. To add to the insanity of the experience, the driver recalled having her radio go haywire and her car's headlights went inexplicably dark—while she drove! The fiery ball was then spotted over the Penobscot River toward Hampden, and flew out of sight. As you could imagine, when one's headlights go off on the road at night, it can be chaotic and scary. In this instance, the witness ended up running her car off the road. Distraught, she sought assistance from nearby homes but found she could not awaken anyone. With her car in the ditch, and emotionally exhausted from her frightening incident, she finally tried to flag down motorists to get a ride home. She also hoped to have someone to share her encounter with and thought they might have seen it as well. She was picked up eventually, and after she related her experience, her rescuer could sympathize but offered that they did not see the fiery ball.

The witness did report her encounter to the FAA, the Bangor police department, and the Orrington town constable, but none had received any reports or occurrences of unusual activity that evening.

In response to the *Strange Maine* article about the encounters, a reader claimed to have also spotted a teal-colored object above a tree line. That sighting occurred in Frenchmen's Bay, Hancock County, Maine, which is approximately forty-eight miles southeast of Orrington. Upon getting as close as possible for a better look at the craft, the witness determined that she may have been mistaken about the object and thought it might have been the lights of a cruise ship. Many ships occupy the harbor during the summer, but despite this, the witness decided to check with the harbormaster the next morning. It was easily discovered that there had been no cruise ships docked in the harbor the previous night. So it would seem that the town of Orrington is not the only place where odd-colored UFOs have been seen amongst the treetops.

A more recent encounter in the dark skies of Orrington occurred on January 13, 2017 (reported by MUFON as "Two Low Flying Triangles Reported Over Maine"). The unnamed witness in this case visited a birthday party for her friend, and soon after their arrival, all partygoers decided to take a trip to Walmart in Brewer. After a bit of fun and shopping, they left the department store at approximately 10:50

p.m. and headed back to Orrington on the Brewer Lake Road. The witness explained, "We had noticed these red lights down the road above the dam on the lake." Since they were still close to Bangor, they first assumed the lights were from an incoming airplane headed to the airport. The sighting of the lights sparked a memory in the witness, about a previous UFO encounter in the area about a year prior, and she told the rest of the passengers of their encounter. While telling the story, the lights of the current sighting made an instant, drastic change in altitude and then flew parallel to the vehicle. The witness wrote, "This triangular silhouette went from being far off the road and fairly high in the air (500-700 feet) to swooping in very close, probably 400 feet off the road and 200 feet high."

They pulled the car over to watch the unusual object, and even tried to record a video of it on one of the passengers' cell phones; however, the video came out too dark. They rolled down the windows but heard nothing from the object. It continued to move, so they started up the car and followed it. As they rounded a bend, a second, larger triangular object was seen. Everyone was shocked by the second craft and thought better of pursuing the objects.

Michelle, on her blog, advises, "If you live in Orrington, perhaps a look upwards now and then would serve the curious among you well!" I would agree wholeheartedly.

INVASION IN SCARBOROUGH

By MUFON's Valerie Schultz and Nomar Slevik

A Maine witness described an encounter with an unidentified object at a drive-in theater in the late summer/early fall of 1975 (MUFON Case #51193).

While in line at the Portland Twin Drive-In Theater in Scarborough, a witness recalled a peculiar event. He said he was "waiting for them to let the cars in, and I noted something to the southeast. It was yellow-orange on the bottom. I didn't think too much about it, but I kept looking that way and it was still there."

The witness first thought it could have been related to the National Guard helicopter training, which he knew occurred near the marsh a few miles away. He'd seen the helicopters before, and the light looked similar, but they never trained over a roadway. The witness continued, "We drove in and parked. About half an hour later I saw it in the south, right by the Scarborough Downs sign about fifty to seventy-five feet off the ground about a mile away. I thought it was strange so I kept looking at it." The object moved toward the witness and the drive-in theater. He watched the object hover right above the shopping center in the area. "I'm thinking what is this? It's going so slow," he proclaimed. "People were looking up and running. Some were dropping their bags. It was close enough for me to see that it was white on top and on the side with square light panels around its bottom that flashed a yellow orange strobe, not in any type of order."

Ten minutes later, the object boldly moved toward the east-facing movie screen. "It was so close I could have hit it with a rock. By now other people are seeing it. Some were pointing at it. It went behind the screen and must have made a ninety degree turn east and came right over the top of the screen about fifteen feet above and just hovered. People were going nuts. Cars were tearing their speakers off! It was just crazy!" The object was silent, and frightened witnesses could not believe the sight before them. Some were screaming.

The object then headed west and hovered in front of the screen for at least five minutes. It was at this point that the witness got a closer look at the strange object. He described it as follows: "It was twenty to twenty-five feet in diameter … the top was white and looked like a capsule from an

Apollo moon mission but there were no markings on it. The bottom part was black and flat with square light panels around it that flashed yellow and orange. There were always three or four lights on at the same time, but not next to each other and not in any particular sequence." Of note: notice the description of the top of this object and its similarity to the Kecksburg UFO case of 1965, and the UFO Jeff saw in Stratton, Maine, as mentioned in the chapter titled "The Woman Who Time Forgot."

The UFO seemed huge against the backdrop of the movie screen and continued to hover. "It never wobbled and seemed to be solid as a rock. It hovered there for at least five minutes. Ten to fifteen cars had remained in the theater with all the turmoil that was going on." The witness said that everyone talked, trying to figure out what the object could be. Some were riveted as it slowly backed away from the movie screen and traveled west on Sawyer Street. It then suddenly changed direction, moved to the north, sped up, and disappeared.

According to the witness, "I wasn't afraid. I think I was in shock. It did not hit me until I got home. To this day if I tell someone the whole story, by the end I am shaking!" He also explained that a local newspaper reported the sighting the next day and, in the witness's opinion, described it falsely as an airplane towing a banner. He thought the report was absurd because he and the other witnesses on-site had heard no sound and observed the UFO hover, and it was disc-shaped, not shaped like an airplane. In total, the witness estimated that eighty to one hundred people had observed the strange object. The chaos of the scene could remind one of an old sci-fi UFO invasion movie.

The sighting was reported to NUFORC and submitted to MUFON. It was investigated by MUFON's State Director for Maine, Valerie Schultz, and closed as "Unknown."

CHASED BY A UFO

Leland Bechtel, retired associate professor of psychology at Bates College and former MUFON State Director for Maine, has researched thousands of UFO cases throughout his career. His work has included many famous cases from the state, such as the Old Orchard Beach incident, rife with men in black visits to Dr. Herbert Hopkins, and the David Stephens case, both written about later in this book. Bechtel has worked with noted Maine UFO investigators and researchers Shirley Fickett, Brent Raynes, and more. Bechtel was always steadfast in his approach to investigations and never turned down an opportunity to reveal the truth, whether big or small. Back in 1984, he investigated an eerie encounter that a young couple from Detroit, Maine, had on the roads of Pittsfield. The following story was reported in the October 1984 edition of the *MUFON UFO Journal* and closed as "Unknown."

In the summer of 1984, America was smitten by the release of the movie *Ghostbusters*. People would see the movie multiple times, and on the night of July 15, Robert White was no different. He was excited to see Venkman and company once again but with girlfriend Carol Cloukey in tow. He'd planned a night of dinner and a movie, and they set out from Detroit toward the theater in Pittsfield. As they drove, they laughed and talked about the day, and then Carol suddenly noticed something odd.

It was an amber-colored light in the sky that seemed, in her opinion, much too bright. She was about to bring it to Robert's attention when she saw the light descend quickly. This motion caught Robert's eye, and the pair drove over sixty miles per hour with the thought that a plane had possibly crashed or lost control. As they got closer, it became obvious that it was not a conventional aircraft. As Robert explained, "It was grayish in color, triangular shaped, and larger than a 747 aircraft. It had four red lights and one or two brighter white lights. It made no sound." The object moved to an altitude of about one hundred fifty feet and hovered above their vehicle. Frightened, Carol shifted the vehicle into reverse and slammed on the gas pedal; Robert could only watch in amazement as they backed away.

The object kept pace along the left side of their car. On the right side of the road, about one hundred yards away, Robert spied a farmhouse and yelled for Carol to back into its driveway. As she did, the UFO continued to pursue them.

Bechtal wrote, "When they stopped the UFO stopped, and when they moved the UFO moved! It became apparent that 'it' did not want to let them go."

Once in the driveway, they both darted from the car, but in opposite directions. Robert yelled for Carol to follow him. As she caught up, a car approached on the main road, and the couple observed the UFO slowly move and hover over a nearby field, which obstructed its visibility from the road. It seemed to them that the UFO was purposeful in that movement, and was hiding from the second car. After a moment, the object vanished, and Robert and Carol were in disbelief. "It disappeared!" exclaimed Robert. "It just seemed to evaporate into thin air." The couple then ran back to their vehicle and hoped the UFO would not return. Thankfully for them, it did not. Nothing else was sighted that evening, and the pair got home, shaken but safe.

In the course of his investigation, Bechtel contacted the owners of the farmhouse, who told him that they had heard a commotion of people outside shouting and running about. They were about to call the police when they observed the couple speed off their property. The owners figured some young kids were having a bit of fun and mentioned that they did not see a UFO or anything out of the ordinary that night. Bechtel also contacted the Bangor Airport, which advised that two Boeing 747 jets did fly over Pittsfield that night. However, the airport confirmed their altitudes to be more than six thousand feet.

During Bechtel's investigation, he found Robert to be a reliable witness. At the time, Robert was a sophomore at the University of Maine, majoring in physical education. Bechtel wrote in his report, "To this investigator, he appears to be reliable, honest, responsible, and intelligent. His parents, likewise, appear to be very responsible, rational, sensitive, and appealing people." During his conversations with Robert's family, he found that two other incidents had occurred a week prior. Robert's brother, an eleven-year-old boy, told his parents that he had seen a large, bright object in the sky above their home in Pittsfield. And Robert's father saw a light streak across the sky while doing yard work.

Bechtel ended his report by stating, "This investigator has complete confidence in the veracity and accuracy of the reporting witness."

THE PSYCHIC WHO SAVED THE WORLD

In 1955, John Anthony Walker enlisted in the Navy. Thirty years later, he was taken into custody by the FBI for espionage. What happened? And what does any of this have to do with unidentified flying objects in Maine? The psychic knows.

It's All About the Benjamins

About thirteen years into his naval career, John Walker experienced financial difficulties in trying to support his wife and four children. He also owned a restaurant that he barely kept in business, and funds were needed badly. One day in 1968 he found himself in Washington, DC, pacing anxiously in front of the Soviet Embassy. He held a closely guarded briefcase and sighed wearily when thinking of its contents. He wiped the sweat from his forehead, looked over his shoulder one last time, and walked inside.

Contained in that briefcase was a radio cipher card. After he spoke with officials inside the embassy, he walked out with a few thousand dollars, a sense of relief, and the beginnings of a torrid double life. That day became the first time John Walker sold US intelligence secrets to the Russians. It also sparked a seventeen-year stint inside an espionage ring that involved friends and members of his own family. He commissioned his wife, Barbara, naval student Jerry Whitworth, his older brother Arthur, and his son Michael, who was an active duty seaman. Walker would eventually try to recruit all his children into the ring, including his youngest daughter, who had recently become pregnant.

Throughout the years, Barbara became despondent over John's involvement with the Russians and despised the fact that he'd recruited his own family members. Her distress turned to anger, and in 1976, they divorced and she moved back to Maine—Skowhegan, specifically. Soon after, Barbara began abusing alcohol due to her constant worry about her children and her ex-husband's espionage exploits. Fast-forward to November 1984, when she finally contacted the FBI office in Boston, Massachusetts, admittedly in an inebriated state. But she did succeed in reporting John's secret activities.

Okay, let's step back for a moment. We finally have a Maine connection with Barbara's move to Skowhegan. So ... UFOs? I know, just be patient with me.

While living in an apartment complex in Skowhegan, Barbara became friendly with the Vigue family. The family's daughter, Shalel, was (and still is) a practicing medium and tarot reader, and she happened to be Barbara's neighbor. One day in January of 1984, Barbara came to Shalel for help. She asked for a reading because she wanted guidance to decide if she should turn her ex-husband in to the authorities. Shalel told the *Washington Post*, "She said she suspected he was giving secrets to the Russians. She said he would get drunk and call her on the phone and brag about it." After much consideration, and specifically crediting Shalel for her guidance, Barbara called the FBI and reported John on suspicion of espionage.

Author Howard Blum wrote of John's exploits in the book *I Pledge Allegiance*. Pick it up if you can. It is a fascinating read.

The Psychic and the Stars

Due to the John Walker story, interest in Shalel's work grew, and she was interviewed by the *New York Times*, *Washington Post*, numerous other major newspapers around the world, and local author C. J. Stevens. In Stevens's subsequent book, *The Supernatural Side of Maine*, he revealed some interesting insights of the extraterrestrial variety. Shalel disclosed that she'd begun speaking to extraterrestrials at the age of twelve. She explained that she could speak with them telepathically, and they made her aware of her psychic abilities.

She described a 1967 encounter where she observed a UFO outside her bedroom window—an orange light. She then saw a face in the clouds that was "long and gaunt." She further explained, "They told me that I had abilities unlike others, and I would be responsible in the coming years for helping the US gain world peace with Russia. I also asked it if this is really what you look like, the extraterrestrial said, 'That's the closest that I can let you see of my real face so you will not be afraid.'" She had two other encounters with this extraterrestrial (1975 and 1977) and was given messages that they meant us no harm. She said, "They are intent on the preservation of our species."

After researching the John Walker case and Shalel's involvement with it, I contacted her for an interview. I met with her in July 2016 at her home in Skowhegan. As I pulled into her driveway, a gorgeous Persian cat greeted me outside. A woman came to the door with a big smile and a warm greeting. As we became acquainted, kittens paraded into the room. Side note—I love kitties! And to be interviewing a UFO witness, conducting research, and surrounded by kittens ... I must tell you, dear readers, I was in heaven! Anyway, let's get back to Shalel.

As a young girl, she had told her parents of her encounters with extraterrestrials. In her opinion, her folks reacted poorly to this revelation. They assumed something must be wrong with their daughter and promptly took her to the hospital. After an examination and tests, the family doctor found nothing medically wrong with Shalel and sent her and her parents on their way. Her mother then figured it must be a spiritual issue and took Shalel to a retreat center in Augusta. As she explained to me, "My mother brought me to the hospital because she didn't know what to think. After all the tests came back negative, and I was found mentally stable, she brought me down to Dedication to the Mary Mother of Jesus at Saint Paul's Retreat Center in Augusta, Maine." Father Val was one of the servicing priests at this retreat center and Shalel's mother had her meet with him. Of note is the fact that Father Val had a Vatican sanction to perform exorcisms, and Shalel's mother thought that might be just what her daughter needed. As Shalel explained, "Father Val had been blessed by the Pope to perform exorcisms, and my mother took me down to verify that I wasn't possessed by demons. He told my mother, 'If she does have a demon, I will exorcise that demon.' He chuckled a bit after my mother left the room. Well, after the Father spoke to me he told me that I was a fine, normal girl and to keep reading." According to Shalel, her mother was a good woman who appreciated both the doctor's and priest's diagnosis, and she supported Shalel's gift.

Cured!

During the ice storm of 1998, there was another otherworldly encounter that resulted in physical evidence, witnessed by one of Shalel's neighbors, and also a miraculous healing for both Shalel and her cat. "I believe the extraterrestrials made the ice storm happen," Shalel explained to me. "They landed on the roof of where I was living [corner of Chandler and Stewart Streets in Skowhegan]. And my neighbor asked me if I believed in UFOs because something had landed on the roof the night before and left an impression in the ice!" Shalel was taken aback by this claim, and both hurried outside to look at the roof. Sure enough, there was a perfect circle melted into the ice! The neighbor speculated that perhaps it was the military or the National Guard running training maneuvers in the area. Shalel gave in to this possibility but knew that something different had been afoot.

During that time, Shalel told me, she'd suffered from a tumor in her adrenal gland and her cat had feline leukemia. On the morning of her neighbor's report, she knew something felt different, and then her neighbor's discovery confirmed it. Weeks before the ice storm began, Shalel had prayed and meditated to everything and anything she could think of to avoid surgery on her tumor. She told me, "I put that out to the universe. If there are angels, if there are saints, if there are loved ones passed on. Or extraterrestrials that 'wanna' help me with this. Remove this adrenal tumor!" Weeks passed with no answer...until the ice storm came. "That morning I woke up and all my pain from the tumor was gone," she exclaimed. "I know that leukemia was gone too. That cat was running around like a kitten, all lit up." Shalel felt great, the best she had in years. No more pain, no more aches, and even her cat seemed renewed and went on to live several additional years.

"I know they made this ice storm to help me with this," Shalel said. "There must be more to this. They're going to use me again. Why go to all this trouble?" I asked, "Use you for what?" "Well, that would bring us to 2009," she replied. "I told you about when I was twelve and they said I would help the US with Russia. That was more than just the Walker case."

Shalel believed her visitations were meant for a greater purpose, and that her visitor's mysterious messages and healings would all culminate in an event she described as "intense and controversial." She anxiously anticipated their next arrival.

The Time Is Upon Us!

About ten years after the ice storm incident, Shalel's extra-terrestrial brethren reappeared once again. She noted that this encounter was different from the others; she had been awaiting this moment and knew it would be significant. The encounter suggested world affairs and avoidance of war but gave her little else to go on. "I woke up one morning after having a vivid dream, or what seemed like a dream," Shalel said. "The one who visits me arrived again and told me something significant." (While Shalel was explaining this to me, her demeanor changed. Not drastically, but it was apparent. She adjusted her seat and her tone lowered. I could tell that I was about to hear something important.) "He said to me, 'The time is upon us, what we trained you for. I'm sorry if it is scary, you really have to rise to the occasion.'"

At this point in the conversation, Shalel looked at me and smiled. She must have seen my receptive demeanor as I actively listened. "I'm going to show you the deck I used," she continued. Shalel uses tarot cards in her readings and meditation to help her receive messages. "It's a world Dakini deck." She splayed the cards across a table in her living room. (I researched the deck when I got home and found that this type of deck is said to show the intuitive wisdom of the "oracle," which helps to find meaning in the unwritten future.)

After her encounter with the extraterrestrial visitor, Shalel meditated and then went through the deck and found "something of interest," as she put it. She said to me, "Then I realized what it was. Ahmadinejad, the president of Iran, had bought a missile from Russia with which to deliver an atom bomb to the state of Israel to wipe Israel off the face of the Earth. He wanted to do this before the election in June because he knew he couldn't win legally. But in case he lost, he wanted to leave a legacy." I looked at her, dumbfounded. My jaw probably dropped, mainly because I couldn't fathom how she'd gotten that from her meditation and the deck. She said, "You have to read them, over and over, put it all together." And put it together she did.

Iran's election in 2009 was filled with controversy. Mahmoud Ahmadinejad was running against three opponents. With 62 percent of the votes counted, Ahmadinejad was announced the victor. This irregularity surprised the people of Iran, which resulted in protests by thousands across every single Iranian city. "I was very interested in the situation in Iran," Shalel said. "I have friends in the area. For years, they have suffered through multiple tyrannies." Concerned after her meditation, Shalel conducted research on Ahmadinejad and searched for verification of the missile purchase.

According to my own research and knowledge of the situation, Iran was in talks with Russia in 2009 about purchasing Soviet surface-to-air missiles, but the deal never went through due to UN sanctions in 2010. It came up again in 2015 when multiple countries, including the United States, condemned the sale. And finally, in 2016, the deal went through and the missiles were delivered. Shalel, however, had unearthed a different version of events when she found a peculiar news report from 2009. As she explained, "In an obscure CNN archive it said 'Iran purchases Missile from Russia.' I went into that story and found that the missile was supposed to be used to deliver an atom bomb to Israel because Ahmadinejad wants them destroyed."

During my research into Shalel's story (summer 2016), I searched the exact terms of the article as she did and received an "HTTP Status 404" error. This type of error means that communication with the server did connect properly, but I found no results due to the original link either having been removed or broken. A common error type, for sure, but it could imply something may have been there previously.

Once Shalel studied the situation, she knew she had to act. She thought about the alien request, her meditation, and what her cards had told her, and she devised a plan. "I found five to six people in my network who are at the top in their field. This includes military officials, masons, and members from the Dalai Lama group. I contacted them, told them of what I found and asked what to do with this information." One of her contacts took great interest in what Shalel had to say. He was a Marine veteran who shared a peculiar dream with Shalel that he felt foreshadowed something. It was about the world being on a tortoise's back, and the world would plummet if not for that tortoise. He felt that Shalel's findings and the extraterrestrial intervention, coupled with his dream, was a call to action.

He asked Shalel, "What makes this Ahmadinejad man tick? We've got to do this from another approach. We've got to get inside his head and get him to change his plan." Shalel pondered this and suddenly it hit her like a ton of bricks. She knew what they had to do. She knew the one thing that would change Ahmadinejad's mind about setting off an atomic bomb on Israel: family. "Let's scare the bejesus out of him by sending military snipers to take out his two sons! We'll contact him and tell him if he doesn't change his mind, his sons will be dead in hours. It's a bluff, but we'll make him believe it." They both thought the idea could work, so they set out to get the ball rolling. Shalel had an Israeli friend whom she'd met online. She told me, "They were from a very wealthy family and had connections to Iraq, Iran, and Israel. His father was an oil baron." With a plan in place to communicate that message to Ahmadinejad, Shalel prayed that it would work. "I prayed on it. I didn't want the world to have to endure this. The extraterrestrials knew and came to me. The radioactive air would affect millions for generations."

Did It Work?

As the date of the election approached, no bombs were dropped. According to Shalel, the plan worked! An atomic bomb was not dropped on Israel, and, Shalel explained, as a final act to preserve his status, "Ahmadinejad rigged the election in 2009 to remain president so he could figure out a different plan for his legacy. But we did it!" I felt her terrific pride in this during our conversation.

It's a wild story, but the emotion was real. I thought about it on my drive back to Bangor. Was the world a better place because of this psychic from Skowhegan? Was she an unsung hero who had had a hand in thwarting a nuclear war? I couldn't begin to fathom this thought, and really, I could have just dismissed her. But if you remember from the "perception" discussion at the beginning of this book, never dismiss the outrageous just because it's easy to. Maybe Shalel did save us, or maybe she didn't. What I do know after meeting and spending time with her is that she'd save the world time and time again if given the chance.

STARSHIP TROOPER

By MUFON's Valerie Schultz and Nomar Slevik

In the mid-1920s, attorney Edward Godfrey procured numerous farms in the Bangor area and set out to build an airfield. In 1927, Godfrey Field was opened and eventually solidified commercial flights from Northeast Airlines. In the early 1940s, as World War II heated up, Godfrey Field was turned into Bangor Army Airfield to assist with war efforts. The field changed its name to Dow Army Field in 1942 in honor of Army Air Corps pilot James Frederick Dow, who was killed in 1940 when he collided with another pilot over New York state. Five years later, when the Army Air Corps had become the United States Air Force, the field's name was changed one last time to Dow Air Force Base. It was in operation until 1968 and then sold to the city of Bangor and turned into a commercial airport, although the Air National Guard does remain on-site.

A former Air Police Officer (airman) who was on duty at Dow during the 1960s described peculiar UFO and alien encounters that he experienced, per testimony in MUFON Case #76253. The following events took place between March 1963 and November 1964.

The airman's first encounter was with odd lights while on duty at the base in March of '63. He told MUFON, "I was stationed as a K-9 Sentry, guarding B-52 alert bombers loaded with nuclear weapons. The site where the bombers were parked was near the 33 end of the runway. It was about 2300 hours (11:00 p.m.), and time for the second shift to start. As the truck pulled up for my relief, I began to muzzle my dog when he broke position and pulled me on the side of the truck facing the runway. Then I saw the three pulsating spheres of light. As they slowly came down the runway (from the 15 end) they paused halfway. The whole base lit up brighter than daylight, but it was not a blinding light. The light was more beautiful than daylight."

The airman called Central Security Control (CSC) to report the incident and found that it had already been seen and reported by tower personnel. The witness remembered that when using his radio to report the orbs of light, there had been a great deal of static that came through. He was approximately seven hundred fifty feet from the orbs at the time and stated, "As I looked up from my radio, the objects, who were three in number, and about thirty feet in diameter each, shot up at a 90-degree angle and turned many colors. They were gone in a matter of seconds."

The witness was unable to observe any structure behind the reddish-orange orbs, and felt that perhaps a cloaking device had been used. He said that the orbs sometimes appeared transparent but was unable to actually see through them. The motion of the colors reminded him of volcanic lava as the red-orange glow moved around the outside of the mysterious spheres. The orbs were pulsating, and although heat waves were visible, the witness did not feel any warmth radiate from them. "The three spheres were in a V formation but opposite the usual formation. There were two in the front and one in the back. When the orbs continued down the runway at the 33 end, it was like they hit a wall, and just went up at a phenomenal speed while spinning and turning many colors."

The witness and other personnel then drove around the perimeter of the base. "The flight leader driving the truck and everyone else were terrified and we sped to CSC and were met by Office of Special Investigations officers (OSI) where they interrogated me for about forty-five minutes. The strange thing was they kept asking me if I knew who and what they are." The witness found their questions quite peculiar, and was eventually told to write a statement about the events he had witnessed. After writing down his observation, he was then forced to sign an affidavit saying he was not to talk about the event while in the service, and that if he did speak about it he would be jailed. This obviously concerned the airman, and he knew that orders were orders, so he kept his silence for over fifty years.

It was also confirmed to the witness that the orbs were captured on radar. He elaborated further: "The 75th ADC Squadron stationed at Dow Air Force Base sent two F-101s after the objects. I was told the 6th Air Division in Pease, New Hampshire and the 8th Air Force Headquarters in Westover, Massachusetts had picked them up on radar. They were also seen the next few nights near the nuclear weapons depot, which was about two miles from the 33 end of the runway." The witness did not hear any sound coming from the orbs but felt that his guard dog could hear something from them since it was agitated for the entire encounter. He estimates this event to have been approximately eight to nine minutes, but could have been a bit longer. "Only years later, I had the feeling that for some reason, time had stood still."

Monsters and Aliens

The airman spoke of a few other encounters while on duty at the base. Sometime during 1963 or 1964, the witness was on duty and resting in a ditch with his trusty companion when his guard dog suddenly went on alert. He had trouble keeping ahold of its leash; the dog wanted to run out of the ditch and up a nearby hill. The witness got out of the ditch quickly to see what had gotten his reliable dog so riled up.

His K-9 counterpart was focused, observing something phenomenal. The witness described seeing a large, bipedal, hairy, humanoid figure at the top of the hill. He thought the beast could have been a Bigfoot-type creature and estimated its height as eight to nine feet tall. Shocked, he could barely move, but studied and marveled at the being. Slowly, he reached for his radio and called his base command to report the odd intruder. The voice on the other end of the radio advised him to not approach the being, and to wait for the base's Six Man Strike Team to arrive. When they showed up, a full investigation of the area was launched. The team could not find the creature, but the witness made sure to write an official report about the incident.

Another event occurred on a late spring evening of 1964. The witness had just started his post and was conducting a security walk-through with his guard dog when it went on high alert again. The dog was focused on a house near the base. As the witness's flashlight lit a basement window of the house, he was startled to see two people hiding inside the basement. The house was located near the Hammond Street gate of the bomber area of the base. He radioed the presence of the intruders to base command, who then sent the Strike Team to investigate. They arrived swiftly and apprehended the individuals. The Strike Team marched the intruders out of the building; it was at this point the airman was able to see the figures. He said, "they were not like regular people," and described them as grayish in color with emotionless faces. He compared the captured pair to the Teros alien species—a subsurface race that was featured in the video "Alien Races A-Z 3rd Edition," which can be viewed on YouTube. (To get there quickly, you can scrub to the 16:57 mark.) Similar to one of the photos in the video, the airman described the individuals as wearing hats and coats; however, their noses were not as exaggerated. The witness was later congratulated for his help in apprehending the pair, but he was never told of their fate.

A few months later, the witness reported more odd lights on the base. These were not described as orbs, but something more like the aurora borealis. The difference was that the prisms of light came all the way down to the ground, and the airman recalled walking through colors of red, blue, and green. After this event, he speculated whether there could be some sort of dimensional opening at the base.

Portals have been described in other areas of the world as well. One in the United States is located at Skinwalker Ranch in Ballard, Utah. NIDSci, which I mentioned in chapter one, conducted a long-term investigation of the ranch. While there, scientists observed Bigfoot-type creatures, UFOs, haunting activity, and even dinosaurs! You can read about the ranch in the book *Hunt for the Skinwalker* by Colm Kelleher and George Knapp. You can also listen to a great podcast about Skinwalker Ranch from Jack Stockwell (December 3, 2014).

During its heyday, Dow Air Force Base was a busy and crucial addition to the Strategic Air Command sector due to its flight line for international aircraft. In the 1960s, it boasted a large cache of nuclear weapons. As UFO researcher and author Robert Hastings put it in his 2006 article about UFO sightings at military sites, "Our nuclear weapons program is an ongoing source of interest to someone possessing vastly superior technology. Significantly, the reported UFO activity occasionally transcends mere surveillance and appears to involve direct and unambiguous interference with our strategic weapons systems."

Another event, unrelated to the witness cited above, was reported in February of 1966 from the National Investigations Committee of Aerial Phenomena (NICAP). They reported in their newsletter, *The UFO Investigator*, that two Skowhegan police officers observed a large, domed, disc-shaped object with an orange, glowing light. Patrolman Robert Barnes and Special Officer Everett Laporte first saw the object while in their cruiser at 11:55 p.m. They called in the sighting to their dispatch, who reached out to the FAA and Dow Air Force Base. Both tracked the mysterious object on radar. The newsletter also stated that the object was "easily visible because of its orange glow, the unknown object slowed down and hovered above the town, going through several maneuvers before it speeded up and disappeared." An FAA spokesman stated that Dow had only reported "an intermittent blip over the Skowhegan-Augusta area." In contrast, the FAA confirmed that the object was "making tight turns at a low altitude, and

Dow personnel apparently were not able to determine if the object was an aircraft or not."

I have spent a lot of time at this former base. It is currently bustling with activity, since it's an operational international airport, which makes an investigation of the area difficult. I did spend some time at the Hammond Street gate but failed to observe anything out of the ordinary.

The airman's observation of the lights, the humanoid figure, and the alien beings were investigated by MUFON's Valerie Schultz. The case was closed as "Unknown."

LORING'S FIRST ENCOUNTER

Loring's history as one of Maine's most beloved Air Force bases has long outlived its closure in 1994. The base was operational for more than forty years, and served as one of the Air Force's largest Strategic Air Command bases during its service. After its closure, it was converted into an industrial commerce park with part of the property utilized by Loring Job Corps. Also, the Department of Defense has an operational Finance and Accounting Services building on-site.

In my first book, I wrote of Loring's thrilling three-night encounter with UFOs in 1975. The story also made its way to an episode of the television show *Close Encounters*. It is episode 8 of season 1, called "Nuclear Reaction," and can be viewed in full on YouTube. The presence of UFOs in and around military bases is a story that has been told countless times, including at Dow Air Force Base in the previous chapter. The connection typically involves bases with nuclear technology on-site. As military UFO researcher Robert L. Hastings wrote, "Air Force, FBI, and CIA files declassified via the Freedom of Information Act establish a convincing, ongoing pattern of UFO activity at US nuclear weapons sites extending back to December 1948."

Recap of the 1975 Encounters

On October 27, 1975, an unidentified flying object hovered in and around Loring Air Force Base. Multiple staff members from the base witnessed the events, including the base's wing commander. The following is a brief description from my first book, *UFOs Over Maine*: "The ship was seen just hovering over the base, and at one point it just disappeared. Moments later, it was hovering one hundred and fifty feet over the base's runway. As numerous base personnel looked on in awe, a plan was made to confront the craft from the ground. The men piled into a truck and started driving down a parallel road to the runway, toward the object. Once they reached the turn to the weapons storage area, the craft was approximately three hundred feet in front of the truck and reportedly only hovering five feet off the ground."

This incident has garnered significant attention, and since then has been dissected not only within ufology, but by locals, journalists, former airmen who were stationed at Loring (before, during, and after the incidents), and the

Air Force. The Francis Malcolm Science Center in Presque Isle, Maine, holds an annual presentation about the incident during the Halloween season. And, I am told, some of the volunteer staff at the Loring Heritage Museum are open to discussing the matter. Unfortunately, I could not confirm this during my visit to the area because the center was closed.

Immediately following the events, the base did claim that their intruders were drug smugglers in helicopters. Yet despite Loring's initial explanation, none of the eye witnesses claimed to have seen a helicopter. In fact, the only helicopters present were from the National Guard, which was stationed at the base and aided in the search, and an Air Force helicopter that was brought in later to assist (on October 30, 1975). The base later conceded to not having an explanation for the UFO. The source of the object remains unknown to this day.

Famed *Bangor Daily News* journalist Dean Rhodes and author-investigator Larry Fawcett found the case intriguing. In 1982 they started an investigation that eventually led them to the FBI offices in Boston, Massachusetts (two years before Barbara Walker reported her husband). Fawcett wrote in a NICAP article, "When Rhodes checked with the FBI in Boston, he was told that the aerial intrusions over Loring remained under investigation and that they had no idea as to who was responsible. A later Freedom of Information request was filed by the authors with the Boston

FBI office, asking for documents concerning the identity of the object. The FBI completely denied any knowledge of the craft or who may have been responsible for the flights." Having exhausted all possible options in their investigation of the incident, Fawcett and Rhodes were left scratching their heads on what was seen over Loring.

The First Encounter

In 2012, Hastings reported that a former airman from Loring came forward to report an incident from 1964, which of course preceded the 1975 event by eleven years. He had been under orders never to speak of the incident and was hesitant to tell his story sooner (sounds like the airman from Dow, doesn't it?). The airman explained, "he told us not to discuss any of it with anyone—ever! The colonel was not in my squadron and I do not remember his name."

The airman went on to explain that on a late October evening (notice that the 1975 incident occurred in October as well—could there be a connection?), while on duty, the airman observed a peculiar object hovering just a few feet above the runway (again, like the 1975 incident). He stated, "I looked toward the end of the runway and noticed an object there. It was not very big, maybe twenty-five to thirty feet wide and ten feet tall or so. It may have been trapezoidal in shape, but I'm not sure. There were no lights on it, and it was dark in color. I had my own cheap 10x pocket scope with me, and when I looked through it at the object, I could see a very slight violet glow coming from its underside. I was about two hundred-fifty to three hundred yards away from the object when I observed it. It was two to three feet above the ground. I don't remember any footpads under it, but I was too far away to be certain. I did not see it land, if it did land. I just happened to look in that direction and it was there."

Moments later, the airman spotted a pickup truck driving down the runway headed toward the object. The type of truck he observed was typically used to "guide aircraft around the flight line." The airman wondered who was inside the pickup, as the Air Police staff typically drove jeeps. When he looked back at the unidentified object, it was no longer there, and then he saw the pickup veer off the runway and out of sight. The airman started walking to the area where the object had been. He spotted another airman nearby and asked him if he had seen the object. The other airman did see the object. As explained by the witness, "He also saw it and said it was black with many flat panels on it. He told me it took off so fast as to be a blur. He was not sure what he saw."

It Came from Outer Space!

The airman also reported another encounter, involving a colleague, from December of '64. It was late at night and the colleague was patrolling his typically assigned B-52 bomber area. The bombers were armed with nuclear weapons and placed on alert so they could be scrambled at a moment's notice. As the airman approached an area behind the bombers, he saw shadowlike figures lurking by a snowbank. He knew no one should be in this area and fired a warning shot. Soon after, he commanded the marauders to turn themselves in. He did not get a response, and the night fell eerily silent after the obnoxious gunfire. He stood reserved and watched for any sign of movement. Suddenly, the figures emerged from the shadows and skulked openly in the moonlight. The airman was frightened by their appearance and fired directly at them. They vanished instantly; he couldn't believe it!

After composing himself, the colleague walked to the area where they'd been and investigated. Unexpectedly, the base came to life. Security lights switched on, and Air Police approached the airman. He was apprehended immediately, and despite his arrest, he could only think "They goddamn vanished!"

He tried to explain his behavior to superiors but was ignored. He was then promptly relieved of duty. They explained to him that firing live rounds on base, without reason and near nuclear weapons, was not only illegal but could be considered treason. They advised him that he was lucky to not serve time in military prison. The original witness explained it as follows: "He was relieved of duty at the time. We all thought he was sleep-walking and woke up startled. He was known as the guy who shot at the 'little green men.' No one took him seriously at the time." Years later, he ran into the disgraced airman and the two briefly discussed the incident. In regard to firing shots at the alleged "little green men," he quoted his colleague as saying, "They were gray, not green."

UFOs & Nukes

Encounters such as the ones described above, and others reported by numerous Air Force personnel (at bases harboring nuclear technology) around the country, could be considered to have some of the most credible eyewitness testimony. The airmen are trained observers and are expected to function while under pressure. This may seem anecdotal, but there are multiple cases reported by seemingly rational military professionals of all rankings, including colonels, wing commanders, and brigadier generals. Given the secrecy that the United States government has been shrouded in since before the latter part of the twentieth century, their information could be considered of the utmost priority. Hastings put it best when he said that "the heightened presence of the UFO phenomenon since the end of World War II is a direct consequence of the advent of the Nuclear Age. To suggest that this is the only explanation for widespread UFO sightings during our own era would be presumptuous, simplistic, and undoubtedly inaccurate. Nevertheless, I believe that the nuclear weapons-related incidents are integral to an understanding of the mystery at hand."

My Overnight Investigation of Loring

On the morning of April 18, 2017, I typed "Loring AFB" into Google Maps and found that Limestone (home of Loring) is a three hour and fourteen minute drive (180 miles) from my home in Bangor. I sighed loudly due to a couple of factors. First, I had just driven to Portland and back on Saturday, April 15, to drop my lovely family off at the Jetport. Second, I had to go back to Portland on April 19 to pick them up. Another long drive in such a short period felt daunting, but realistically, it's not that far. I had been planning the trip to Loring all month, which finally culminated in heading up to the "county" on April 25.

Loring Air Force Base.

An aircraft hangar at Loring Air Force Base.

In preparation, I put together the same gear I'd brought with me to Hacker's Hill, booked a hotel room in the area (Presque Isle), and swapped out batteries and charged my gear. Also, I proceeded to download about ten episodes of the *Flip the Table* podcast that my friend Chris has been producing for the last five years. According to their website, *tableflipsyou. com*, it's a podcast "about the other side of board games." They take a humorous and interesting approach to dissecting funny and obscure board games such as Heartthrob, The McDonald's Game, and more. There's a whole lot of space up north, and my audio companions would be needed.

I left my house at about 9:00 a.m. and my first stop was at the Mount Katahdin overlook right off Interstate 95. After taking the obligatory pictures, I hopped back into my Ford Escape and vowed that my next stop would be Houlton. It was not. I stopped at a rest area further north and vowed again to make no more stops until Houlton. I did it! I then pulled into the Maine State Police Barracks on Route 1 and told them of my plan to hang out at Loring Air Force Base at ungodly hours. They politely thanked me, but advised me to inform the local PD instead. Fair enough. I reached Presque Isle at around 12:30 p.m. and checked into my hotel (thank goodness for early check-ins!). I freshened up a bit, then headed to Limestone. I walked into the municipal building and explained to the officer behind the counter about my otherworldly intentions on the base. He took down my information and thanked me for letting them know.

I finally reached the base at around 1:30 p.m. I was utterly unprepared for how desolate and abandoned the place felt. Roadways were cracked from vegetation, and the former military housing area would be the perfect setting for *The Walking Dead*. Large hangars were fatigued and bled rust, and the runways felt massive and like they were from another decade. I looked inside buildings through broken windows and took hundreds of pictures. I made sure to stake out the areas that I wanted to visit later that evening, and noted how to get back to them come nightfall. I left the base around 3:30 p.m. and got a bite to eat. I napped afterwards, called my girlfriend (she wished me luck and told me to be careful), and headed back out at 9:30 p.m.

I arrived on-site at around 10:00 p.m. and was surprised at how different the base was at night. There were absolutely no lights (I don't know why I thought there would be). The only signs of life were from the Loring Job Corps campus, but once I left their grounds, the base swallowed me completely. I was lost for about twenty minutes as I searched for Tower Road. This is the area that gets you to the radar tower and the runways. My plan was to hang out on the runway for a while, as it had an unobstructed view of the sky. After utilizing Google Maps again, I found my way to the areas I wanted to investigate.

I parked awkwardly in what I considered the center of the area, shut off all lights and the car, and watched the skies. It was drizzling that evening, and after about an hour, the rain sounded like white noise and I was in total darkness. I began to feel claustrophobic. The irony was not lost on me, given the fact that I was in the widest of open spaces. I started my vehicle but soon exited it, hoping to feel lighter. I was still surrounded by darkness, but the glow from my dash lights, the fresh air, and the rain hitting my face helped me feel better. I lit a cigarette and continued to watch the skies.

After a moment, I could hear someone walk down the runway. It was faint, but it sounded like they would take a few steps, pause, and then take a few more steps. I wondered whether they walked in this manner to avoid detection. I strained my eyes in an effort to see who or what was approaching, and, I'll admit, I was frightened. I stepped in front of my vehicle, which was still running—and was relieved to figure out that the sound was coming from my intermittent windshield wipers. Whew! I thought I might have been losing my mind.

After laughing at myself, I got back in the car and headed toward the hangar just opposite Tower Road. This thing was a behemoth, and in the darkness it felt as though it was three hundred feet tall (it wasn't). I parked near its entrance and used the light from my full-spectrum camera screen to light my way. I took some pictures and had a brief EVP session by the open door. I then got back into my vehicle, shut everything down, and watched the skies once again. I considered some UFO summoning, like I'd done at Hacker's Hill, but decided against it since I hadn't been on-site for very long. Midnight approached, and I decided to drive to the parking lot of the radar tower to watch the skies from that vantage point.

Once I had parked, my head was on a swivel. On the runway and at the hangar area, the view is completely unobstructed. You can simply see the entire sky. But in the tower's parking lot, you have to scan the area from left to right to see everything. Just after midnight, as I was looking into the sky toward my left, my head coming back to the right, I noticed a light in the sky. With camera already in hand, I immediately turned it on and hit record. After about thirty seconds, I decided to try to drive closer to the light. It seemed impossible to gauge where it was in the sky, as I couldn't even see the radar tower in the darkness. I drove forward about five feet when the light suddenly flashed, shimmered briefly, and then blinked out.

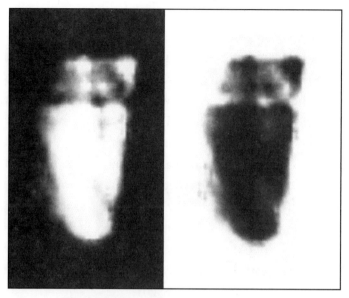

Close-up of my photo of a potential Loring UFO.

I was frustrated in that moment and mad at myself for moving the vehicle. Despite this, when I played back the footage, I found that I'd captured the entire series of events! Honestly, the video simply shows a light in the sky, a flash, and then nothing. Nonetheless, a true unidentified light was captured. I turned on my headlights to see where the tower was in relation to the light. I was surprised to find how far left, and low, the tower was in comparison to where the light was situated. In the darkness, it had felt like they were next to each other, and my skeptical mind thought it was a reflection at first. If I had to guess, I would say the light was about three hundred feet in the air.

I stayed at Loring for another two hours or so before departing. I drove back to the runways, visited an abandoned building, and skulked about the property without further incident. During this time, I uploaded the video to Facebook. The LTE service was weak and it took almost an hour and a half to upload. I arrived back at the hotel at around 3:00 a.m. and began analyzing the footage. It wasn't all that compelling, so I took a screenshot of the light and zoomed in. There is an implied structure within the light, but it's difficult to discern any real detail. I have included the close-up pictures, along with the video, in a high-resolution version uploaded to my YouTube channel ("Nomar Slevik"). You can also find it by searching for "Light in the Sky over Loring AFB—April 26, 2017."

What's the final verdict on Loring? How about we first revisit what has taken place so far. There were reports of a UFO and odd figures on the base in 1964. We know that in October 1975, the United States Air Force confirmed that the base had had intruders in its air space and that it had spanned three nights. And lastly, we have a light in the sky that I observed in 2017. To answer the question of whether Loring Air Force Base has been visited by otherworldly vehicles and alien beings is impossible. Skeptics will say no, and believers will say yes, so what are we left with?

Well, the only thing I know for sure is that you should take the time to travel to Limestone, Maine, and see this historic base for yourself. It truly is something to behold. And while you're there, maybe you'll see something for yourself.

UFO ODDMENTS

Was it Maine's Roswell? Well, not really. No crash was reported. However, I like to call it that, since in the same year and month (and close to the same day) of the now infamous Roswell crash in New Mexico, a fleet of UFOs was reported in Maine's skies.

Maine's Roswell

From July 3, 1947, comes a report from the small coastal town of Harborside. The witness was John Cole, an astronomer from South Brooksville, Maine. He said that at 2:30 p.m. one afternoon, he observed no less than ten UFOs moving northwest across the sky above him. In the book *Our Brothers in the Skies: The Hidden Truth Revealed* by M. R. Fluet, Mr. Cole speaks of what he observed: "Ten very light objects, with two dark forms to their left, moved like a swarm of bees to the northwest. A loud roar was heard."

The Seavey Brothers' Encounter

Wendell Seavey, a fisherman from the small coastal town of Bernard, is the seventy-five-year-old author of the book *Working the Sea: Misadventures, Ghost Stories, and Life Lessons from a Maine Lobsterman.* In it, Wendell Seavey describes an encounter with an unknown oddity in the sky while fishing with his brother in August of 1966.

"It was a dark clear night," he writes. "We were the only boat traveling out from Bass Harbor at that time, all alone out there." He was steering the boat and saw the object before his brother did. "I can't say just how high, but maybe 1,000 feet up, maybe 1,500 into the sky, I saw—knowing not what else to call it—a spaceship." Frank, Wendell's brother, finally saw the object and said it was gigantic, and, having seen the movie *Close Encounters of the Third Kind*, that it was similar in size and shape. Wendell then explained the UFO's peculiar behavior: "Right out of the center of the bottom of it, there came a big shaft of light—a spotlight—and they were shining that light down on the island of Placentia."

This was not the first time Wendell had seen odd lights in the sky, but it was the first time he had seen an object associated with them. While it was odd, he was not frightened and decided to show off. "Like a damn fool, rather than stay there and watch and study and observe it, I had to get smart. Thinking about what I had done on previous occasions and unable to resist showing off, I said to Frank, you want to see your little brother make them shut down that light?" Frank, in disbelief, agreed to his brother's antics, and Wendell flashed the boat's running lights on and off about three or four times. Sure enough, the UFO responded by shutting off the beam of light, as well as the lights on its underside, and then it vanished! Both Wendell and Frank were astonished by this, but duty called and they continued to their fishing grounds. After a few minutes, they turned to look at where the UFO had been … It was back, with all its lights on including the spotlight.

A big thanks to Michelle Souliere for bringing this story to my attention.

Shirley Fickett: UFO Hunter

Shirley Fickett and her husband were the owners of the Driftwood Art Gallery & Gift Shop in Portland, Maine. Shirley was also active in ufology and involved with local sighting research and investigations. She held gatherings at her gallery where one was encouraged to discuss UFOs, ghosts, psychic abilities, and other paranormal phenomena. Sadly, she passed away in 2005. Loren Coleman, owner and curator of the International Cryptozoology Museum, said in memoriam that "Shirley was the Dean of Ufology in the Pine Tree State, Maine's answer to Betty Hill."

Shirley Fickett was instrumental in bringing the Herbert Hopkins-David Stephens case to light in the 1970s and wrote an extraordinary report for the *Flying Saucer Review* journal called "The Maine UFO Encounter: Investigating Under Hypnosis." Her report, along with connected articles by Brent Raynes and Dr. Berthold E. Schwarz, can be read in full in Dr. Schwarz's book *UFO Dynamics: Psychiatric and Psychic Dimensions of the UFO Syndrome*. If you have trouble finding a copy of Schwarz's book, you can do a search for Shirley Fickett's article title on Google, where you will find a PDF version of *Flying Saucer Review*. That said, a retelling of the Herbert Hopkins-David Stephens case appears in my first book, *UFOs Over Maine: Close Encounters from the Pine Tree State*.

The Curious Case of Earl Whitney

Brent Raynes, UFO investigator and researcher, reported that on the afternoon of Wednesday, June 3, 1970, fifty-two-year-old Earl Whitney was killed by a lightning strike on the golf course at the Augusta Country Club. Before this tragedy, Whitney was known for reporting UFOs on numerous occasions. One of Whitney's last reported cases was an interesting event that involved a landed UFO. Brent Raynes explains that "in the fall of 1945, outside an airport in Waterville, Maine, [he] had observed the landing of a craft that resembled two aluminium pie plates attached lip to lip, with a dark band around the center. He said that this was around 11:00-11:30 p.m., that the UFO had two bright spot lights on the underside, that it landed on four landing legs, remained on the ground for 5-10 minutes, and that afterwards he found impressions on the ground left by the four legs."

Star-Crossed Lovers

In September of 2016, Audrey Hewins (founder of Starborn Support, an alien abduction support group foundation located in southern Maine) announced on her Facebook page that she and Travis Walton of *Fire in the Sky*: *The Walton Experience* fame are now in a relationship. (Travis's story is one of the most compelling alien abduction cases, rivaling Whitley Strieber and the Betty and Barney Hill case.) Audrey wrote on her page, "Brought together by forces well beyond our understanding. It has not been easy as the dark ones do not want us together, but I assure you, after their best attempts to fracture us, we only grew stronger." I, for one, wish them all the joy in the world.

Audrey's story can be seen on a television episode of *Alien Encounters* from the BIO channel. A quick search on YouTube will allow you to view the episode in full.

Travis Walton and team released a great documentary called *Travis: The True Story of Travis Walton*. Also, an amazing retelling of Travis's story was made by Syfy's *Paranormal Witness* television program, also available on YouTube in full.

Palermo Ball Lightning

A gentleman by the name of Merton Haskell told some peculiar stories from the 1930s about odd encounters that he and his parents had experienced in Palermo, Maine. Brent Raynes reported on the encounters and interviewed Haskell. The man claimed that he and his folks were in a neighbor's field when they suddenly noticed odd, bright, pulsating balls of light just over the field. Raynes recorded Haskell as stating that "in a field of crops on our neighbor's field," he "was cultivating the rows with a team of horses and a two-row cultivator when the horses approached it." Haskell went on to explain that at first his father didn't see the lights until they moved closer to the cultivator. "Apparently neither he nor the animals saw it. As they passed over it, it grew smaller until about the size of a baseball and from where we were standing, two hundred yards plus, it rolled with the dirt around the cultivator teeth and (then) immediately resumed its former pulsing size."

Raynes reported another story that Haskell told of odd lights on the night his grandfather passed away. Haskell said, "The last time anyone ever saw it was the night my grandfather died and it was sighted by my father on a stone wall, a line between our farm and the next, this was the closest it ever got to our property. It was never seen by anyone after that."

Ball lightning is a natural phenomenon created during thunder and lightning storms, typically from cumulonimbus clouds. This phenomenon has also been reported during crop circle formations, before and after the death of a loved one, or as ghostly lights seen in a field, bog, or swamp and often called will-o'-the-wisp.

The Teacher Who Didn't Believe

In his book *New England's Visitors from Outer Space*, author Robert Ellis Cahill shares an anecdotal story from 1984.

Arthur Hansen was teaching school at the North Yarmouth Academy in Yarmouth, Maine. During a discussion with his class one day, the topic of extraterrestrials and UFOs was brought up by a student. Mr. Hansen exclaimed to the entire class, "I will believe only if one drops in front of my house on Princess Point Road!" The proclamation started an eruption of laughter and the incident was soon forgotten.

About a week later, the teacher was at home finishing dinner with his family when a knock sounded at the door. Mr. Hansen went to greet his unknown visitor and was shocked to see two of his students quite afraid and ranting about "lights in the sky." Arthur's two sons overheard the reference to a UFO, and all five excitedly hurried down the driveway and onto Princess Point Road to catch a glimpse. Mr. Hansen recounts, "We looked up and were startled and convinced that what we were looking at was very unique." As they approached an area just off the side of the road, strange red lights were visible. As they continued walking, a craft appeared about thirty feet in the sky and the Hansen boys were, as Arthur put it, "frightened and overwhelmed."

Soon after arriving on-site, snickering could be heard coming from the youngsters. Arthur thought this peculiar and looked around the area. He spotted poles by nearby trees that shot straight up into the craft, and upon closer inspection of the craft itself, he could now see that flashlights were wrapped in red nylon that produced the eerie illumination. Once he realized what was really going on, everyone ended up having a good laugh together. The student pranksters, after having heard Mr. Hansen's disbelief in UFOs the previous week, couldn't help but try to make a believer out of him. It backfired, but it was all in good fun.

Maine Signs (Crop Circle Reports)

Crop circles were observed in a field in the Rockland area from 2006 to 2008. The circles in 2007 and 2008 were not investigated, but I did reach out and correspond with a crop circle investigator, who told me that these circles were "almost certainly what we call a 'randomly downed' area, very likely weather-related." Apparently, in similar areas that have been tested, some cases do indicate that the cause was "the same plasma energy system involved in the creation of genuine geometric events," but most areas "do not show the physical abnormalities in the plants associated with crop circle creation. Instead [they're] almost certainly related to either over-fertilzation (when it's a crop field) or weather conditions."

The circle in 2006 was reported by the BLT Research Team as "partially-circular, partially randomly-downed grasses." Witnesses recalled that a thunder-and-lightning storm had occurred the night before. One resident of Rockland who lives near the field reported observing balls of light (BOLs) in the area. The witness did attempt to use a camera in the area of the circle but reported that it would not work. BOLs have been reported all over the world, some having been recorded on video showing the creation of a crop circle. The most famous, or infamous, rather, would be the Oliver's Castle crop circle footage. Conduct a quick search on YouTube to watch the video.

Other reports from around Maine include Turner in 1959, Palermo in 1965 and 1967, Masardis in 1993, Cape Elizabeth in 1997, and the Pittston/Gardiner story from 2002 that I wrote about in my first book.

The 1959 Turner crop circle report also included a witness observing balls of light. The report states, "A small circle of flattened, 'scorched' grass was discovered in a field after a woman standing in her driveway heard a humming sound—then watched several BOLs flying low over a field about 1,000 feet away. The woman reported that BOLs stopped flying and began to hover in midair, and then descend into the field. The circle was found where the BOLs had landed."

The Beasts of Palmyra

Linda Godfrey wrote in her book *Real Wolfmen: True Encounters in Modern America* of a terrifying night in 2007 that befell the Palmyra home of Eric and Shelly Martin. After having just moved into their new house, they were home one evening unpacking and talking about their day when a light outside caught Eric's eye as he walked past a window. He stopped and peered out into the woods and observed BOLs that floated in and out of the trees. By the time Shelly got to the window, the BOLs had disappeared. They thought hunters with flashlights were to blame and continued unpacking. Suddenly, footsteps and scratching sounds were heard coming from their front porch. Eric went to the window, and at first glance thought there was a pack of dogs outside. But they looked much too large to be ordinary dogs and he feared that they might be wolves. He looked at his wife with unsettled eyes and peered out the window again. An onslaught of goose bumps covered his skin as he called his wife to the window. Five extremely large wolf-like creatures stood bipedally and stared back at them. The couple reported that some of them were as tall as seven feet! Throughout the rest of the night, the wolves skulked around their property and tried to break in; Eric described them as having "frightening intelligence." The couple had guns, but they were stored in a shed … outside. All they could do was stay locked inside their home until the creatures retreated, which happened once daylight broke.

Their story was also featured in an episode of *Paranormal Witness* on the Syfy channel and can be viewed in full by searching for "The Wolf Pack Paranormal Witness" on YouTube.

SHOOT LOW, THEY'RE RIDING SHETLANDS

On December 29, 2014, the CIA released a statement via Twitter that read, "#1 most read on our #Bestof2014 list: Reports of unusual activity in the skies in the '50s? It was us." Thus began another wave of what some UFO researchers would call a "disinformation campaign." Essentially, the CIA, in one fell tweet, discounted thousands of UFO reports and witnesses by claiming that all UFO activity reported through the 1950s was due to spy planes. Many of those cases were investigated by Project Blue Book and have remained unexplained by the US government to this day.

Below are some reports from the skies of Maine during that period. These various reports were compiled from

NICAP, MUFON, and the books *Wonders in the Sky: Unexplained Aerial Objects from Antiquity to Modern Times* by Jacques Valle and Chris Aubeck, and *Our Brothers in the Skies: The Hidden Truth Revealed* by M. R. Fluet.

September 16, 1952

Portland. The crew of a US Navy P2V Neptune patrol plane observed, via sight and radar, five lights in the early evening sky. They were tracked on radar for over twenty minutes and remain unidentified to this day.

January, 1953

Presque Isle Air Force Base. A former sergeant at Presque Isle AFB recalled a UFO incident from the early 1950s in which a UFO was observed on radar during daylight hours. The base scrambled four F-94B fighter jets to its last known location. The pilots were able to lock onto a target; however, the object was seen accelerating to over 2,000 mph and ascended to 75,000 feet, thus they lost sight of it.

Another encounter from Presque Isle AFB, that same year, was observed by multiple witnesses. A sergeant who was attempting to bring in his B-26 aircraft observed an unknown object traveling near "Quaggie Joe," a small mountainous area near the base. The sergeant called the sighting into the tower to see if they could confirm the object on radar. The tower confirmed the object, so the B-26 abandoned its landing procedures and followed the object.

The sergeant followed it onto the base as it hovered over the runway. He was then ordered to land his aircraft. During that time, a tower operator took several photographs of the object before it accelerated off at high speed, making a high-pitched noise as it left the area.

Soon after the encounter, all witnesses were interviewed separately, the photos were confiscated, and all were ordered to not speak about what they witnessed.

April 23, 1954

Pittsfield. Mr. and Mrs. F. E. Robinson spied a disc-shaped object with a dome and flashing lights during a morning walk. They said it "made a sound like a swarm of bees" as it hovered just above the treetops. It then took off at great speed.

April 24, 1954

Hartland. Oddly enough, Mr. Robinson spotted a large, silver, oblong object. He explained that it had a dome on top and flashing lights. He observed it for fifteen minutes or so, and then it "flew straight and level and then straight up."

November 15, 1954

Augusta. A manager at radio station WFAV claims to have seen what he described as "ten gold, circular objects that flew in a vertical V formation." He said the encounter lasted approximately three minutes.

December 21, 1955

Washburn. A young woman named Roberta Jacobs was just turning in for the night when a light outside caught her eye. She peered out the window for a better look and saw something quite strange: "a red-orange glow in the moonless and the starless sky." The glow got brighter and was beautiful. She continued to watch this light when the glow dimmed and a UFO-like ship was visible. It was "a disc surmounted by a cupola, giving it an egg-shaped appearance." Roberta was entranced by the sighting and could not look away. The craft then descended enough to hover directly over her barn. Roberta observed that the undercarriage of the object rotated at high speed, and the color of it seemed to change to a pure gold.

Roberta gasped as she saw something else: "Between the bottom of the object and the cupola, a shadow could be seen, moving against the glow." She immediately felt sick and had the sense that "the occupants of the craft were observing her and reading her thoughts." At this point, she was about to call the police, but immediately the UFO ascended at great speed. She reported the incident to police the next day.

November, 1956

Glen Cove. Dr. Andrija Puharich, a physician and noted parapsychologist, had a peculiar encounter along with some friends one evening.

During the visit, they all observed a "ball in the sky," which was initially thought to be the moon until it started moving. Shocked, they watched until it was no longer in sight.

Later that night, the doctor couldn't sleep and went for a walk on the beach. While there, he claims to have seen "a transparent object" and added that it contained "three small figures staring at me." He reported his sighting to his friends the next morning and to local authorities days later.

August, 1959

Turner. Emily Deneault had just arrived home one beautiful August evening. When she got out of her vehicle, she heard a low rumbling sound and witnessed lights hovering over a field across the street. She saw the lights move slightly and thought it could have been a helicopter in distress about to make an emergency landing. But it did not land. It continued to hover. She called for her family to come out and see the oddity. Just as they came to see what the commotion was about, the craft slowly and quietly landed in the field. The lights on the craft turned off. The family could only stare on in disbelief. Just then, another object descended rapidly and hovered directly above the first craft!

Emily grabbed binoculars, but her eyes were blinded by a bright blue light that made her eyes water. Suddenly, the landed object rose off the ground, appeared to join the other, and in an instant they ascended rapidly and out of sight. The family walked over to the field and observed a small area of burnt grass. They alerted the authorities, though no formal investigation was launched.

Updates to Previous Stories

The old phrase "If at first you don't succeed, try, try again" is one I'm comfortable with and lately have fully submerged myself in. The UK website *The Phrase Finder* traces the saying back to the 1800s and identifies it as an American proverb by teacher Thomas H. Palmer. He wrote the proverb in his *Teacher's Manual*: "'Tis a lesson you should heed, try, try again. If at first you don't succeed, try, try again."

Since the publication of my first book, *UFOs Over Maine*, I have learned a few tricks about researching and interviewing UFO witnesses, and more about the nuances of journalism, writing, and publishing. I have improved my research methods to minimize dead ends and unresponsive witnesses, and benefitted greatly from advice from fellow authors, tips from leaders in ufology, and investigative persistence in general.

So it was with renewed bravado that I cracked my knuckles and looked back at some of the famous cases in Maine through this new lens. The following stories, which were discussed in my first book, are revisited in the next four chapters:

- Herbert Hopkins, the famous medical doctor and spiritualist from Old Orchard Beach who had mysterious men in black encounters in 1976. The update on Hopkins includes some damning evidence of a hoax by way of his nephew.

- The John King incident from 1966. This update includes more detailed information about King's encounter and of another UFO landing that occurred thirty days later that shares some similarities. Also, I have since found out that I live less than a mile from Mr. King's encounter—whoa!

- David Stephens's abduction case from 1975. Since publishing the first story, I have gained some additional insight from one of the original investigators, Brent Raynes. He and I corresponded about the case, and he shares some of the thought processes he had during his time interviewing Stephens.

- The Allagash Abductions, 1976. New information has come out from one of the abductees from this famous Maine case that casts doubt on the validity of the four men's abduction claims. From infighting to public dissonance, three of the four abductees are sticking to their story.

THE HOPKINS HOAX

The following includes an update to my story "Doctor's Warning," originally featured in *UFOs Over Maine: Close Encounters from the Pine Tree State.*

The Recap

In my first book, I wrote about Dr. Herbert Hopkins's men in black experience from 1976. The story goes that during the time when Dr. Hopkins was treating alien abductee David Stephens through hypnotic regression therapy, he was visited by a mysterious man in black. The doctor's visitor was quite an odd character who was devoid of all visible hair, including eyebrows; displayed peculiar behavior such as slowed, almost mechanical speech; and at one point proclaimed that his energy had run low.

His stated reason for the visit was to warn the doctor to stop treating David Stephens and to destroy all records having to do with the case. He then threatened the doctor with what could be described as a paranormal parlor trick. He had him hold a coin in his hand and advised him to watch it. After a moment, the coin became blurry and disappeared completely. The visitor then told the doctor that what happened to the coin would happen to his heart should he not comply. Understandably terrified, Dr. Hopkins followed the orders. But he and his family continued to be plagued by men in black visits and UFO sightings for several weeks.

John, Dr. Hopkins's son, had an odd encounter with uninvited guests while at home one afternoon. The visitors wore all black clothing and questioned John and his wife about how humans behave. This included questions and gestures of a sexual nature. And just like that, the visitations ceased.

However, was there more to this odd series of events? Further research into the matter has begun to cast doubt on my belief in Hopkins's story.

The Update

In 2008, there were several blog posts from the nephew of the doctor. His name was Howard Hopkins, and he wanted to set the record straight about his uncle's encounter. Before we fully dive in, it should be said that Howard Hopkins passed away in 2012 at the age of 50. He was a well-known Maine author of numerous Western and horror books. He also authored the Chloe Files, a book series that gained him readers beyond his original writings. I had a unique opportunity to speak with a family member, which I will get into later.

Dr. Herbert Hopkins's story first garnered national attention in the 1970s after being published in the *Star* tabloid. His tale was also told in the Time-Life *Mysteries of the Unknown* book series. Because of the doctor's reputation, the story went viral in its day and appeared in hundreds of books, magazines, and television shows. In his blog, Howard referred to Dr. Hopkins as brilliant: "He was brilliant and the world was better for him. But sometimes that brilliance has its price, or takes its toll." Howard went on to explain the unfortunate real-life story behind his uncle's tale and the real-world tragedies that alcohol and drugs can bring to a family. I would like it noted that I am not including this story to sensationalize it; rather, I only ever want to share the truth, as delicate as that may sometimes be. It becomes even more important when discussing the topic of UFOs. I would rather err on the side of being truthful to a fault. I hope you think that is fair.

Howard explained in his blog that his uncle, though well-meaning, spiraled out of control during the time frame when he reported the man in black encounter. He said that Dr. Hopkins was going through a tumultuous time in his life and had begun drinking heavily. Also, Dr. Hopkins was fascinated by 1950s sci-fi pulp stories, and this is where the doubt in the account begins to take shape. Howard wrote, "My uncle was an avid reader of '50s horror and sci-fi comics, paperbacks and old pulps and minimal research will turn up the parallels. My uncle was, unfortunately, a fantasy-prone individual, craved the center of attention and limelight and on a base level he sometimes just made things up—no matter how hyperbolic—to top everybody else. As brilliant as he was in many areas, however, he was unskilled at fiction." He said that his uncle drank a lot during much of the 1970s and 1980s, spending the evenings with a "magnum of wine," and told of awaking several times in the pre-dawn hours to the sound of his uncle stumbling up the stairs and cursing the "goddamn dog"—a dog who was in actuality next to Howard on his bed.

This is a sad commentary. However, I feel Howard craved the same truth-seeking that I do, as he explained here: "The whole thing was sold to the *Star* and propagated throughout many legitimate journals devoted to psychic and unusual phenomena investigation. Mostly based on a doctor's reputation, despite the obvious inconsistencies of the tale."

Howard also shared many happy moments about his uncle and family. He lived with Dr. Hopkins for a time and loved spending holidays there. He adored his uncle's wife, and spent many days listening to Dr. Hopkins tell stories from the mundane to the fantastic. But he also told of his uncle's distaste for stupidity and said that he was often condescending to people, including family, should their stupidity cross his path. Howard wrote about long lectures his uncle would give him when he was young and got into trouble.

One of Dr. Hopkins's children, John, had an encounter with the men in black along with his wife, Maureen, as mentioned above. Unfortunately, their lives took on tragedies of their own. John's encounter began just as oddly as his father's, when John received a phone call from someone who claimed to know him, who wanted to visit. John went to pick up this person along with his female companion. He did not recognize them, but brought them back to his home regardless. What followed was a bizarre series of questioning and inappropriate sexual behavior. Howard writes, "The truth is again pretty obvious and simple. But unfortunately mixed with family sadness.... At the time, we kids weren't privy to what went on there, but later John told me. John and Maureen were swingers.... It was fairly common for other couples to be coming and going about that place."

This is a startling revelation. John and his wife played a big role in the original story, and to hear this crumbles the legitimacy of the original story further.

John eventually moved to Florida with his wife and mother. One day after their arrival in Florida, John called Howard asking to come stay with him in Maine for a few days for a visit. He agreed, but John and his family never showed up! Howard sadly explained that John was addicted to narcotics and alcohol, and Maureen was involved in recreational drugs and drinking as well. He wrote that John "had terminal liver damage from all the drugs, which he had finally kicked. We expected him and his mom the next week. And never heard from him again. Maureen—in a story I don't really know all the reasons for—shot and killed him in their backyard."

Wow. Here we have the story of a "swingers" couple, who unexpectedly moved out of state, which ends in murder! Another sad event in the Hopkins family timeline.

The original man in black side of the story makes for an intriguing tale and certainly makes one pause. However, Howard's version is sad, tragic, and ultimately most likely the truth in regard to otherworldly matters. I am not trying to slight the work of Shirley Fickett, Raynes, and others. I say this because Howard was there, in Dr. Hopkins's life and in John's life; he had firsthand knowledge.

I thought that perhaps others could help shed some light. I spent quite a bit of time corresponding with a family member close to Howard, who told me, "Personally, I believe Uncle Herb. The man was a very odd duck; however, he was brilliant. He was a lot of things, but not a liar. The rest of the family thought he was batshit crazy. But I will say, Howard was fastidious in his research. . . . There are a lot of things that Howard believed in but there is much he did not . . . " I got the impression that that while Howard genuinely wanted to believe his uncle, he just couldn't. He formed this opinion based on all that he witnessed while living with Dr. Hopkins.

So, what does this ultimately mean for the Herbert Hopkins story? Is it a hoax? Do we have to go back to the drawing board? Not me. I do have an opinion. I will say, like

Howard, I wanted to believe Dr. Hopkins's story and I did for a while. I'm a sucker for a great men in black tale. But after reading Howard's blog, corresponding with the family member, and truly analyzing what is at the heart of the Herbert Hopkins case, I'd have to say that I believe this to be a hoax. This is conjecture at best—that is not lost on me. Regardless, I am entitled to an opinion.

JOHN KING AVENGED!

The following includes an update to my story "Shots Fired!," originally featured in *UFOs Over Maine: Close Encounters from the Pine Tree State.*

The Recap

In my first book, I wrote about John King, a man who came across a peculiar object as he drove on Mount Hope Avenue in Bangor, Maine. I wrote, "Mr. King was immediately snapped out of his happy-go-lucky state of mind when he observed a large, silver-domed disc hovering just a few feet over the road in front of him." In conducting research for this book, I discovered a bit more to the story, as well as information about another encounter that occurred exactly thirty days later in Bingham, Maine. The two stories share some commonalities. I will begin with King's encounter first.

The Update

It was late March of 1966 when John King drove along Mount Hope Avenue. During that time, the area included a swampy field near the Bangor Memorial Hospital. When King drove past the field, he was startled to see an overturned car. He slammed on his brakes, threw the gear shift into park, and jumped out to assist a fellow motorist since no emergency vehicles were yet on scene. He negotiated the marshier sections of the swamp and finally noticed that what he had seen from the road was not a car at all. The *Bangor Daily News*, in an interview with King, provided the following description of what he'd observed: "it was a luminous object hovering over the ground. It was an elliptical object, 6-7.5m diameter, with domed top which had a central yellow-orange light, a blue light to its right, a white light to the left."

This frightened King and sent him running from the object, back to his vehicle. He stopped just before getting inside the car and observed the UFO rock back and forth. King described the movement this way: "The thing began rocking from side to side and began to approach within 60m scraping the elderberry bushes as it did so." Panicked, he reached for a .22 revolver that he had in his vehicle and accidentally fired it off due to his agitated state. The UFO seemed unfazed by the gunshot and continued to approach. This time King aimed carefully and fired. Unfazed, the UFO kept moving toward him. He fired a third time when suddenly the UFO glowed bright and shot up into the sky. He took the opportunity to jump into his vehicle and flee the area. He went to the authorities and explained his odd encounter. With directions from King, police searched the area and found a scorched area of vegetation. Despite this bit of evidence, the police dropped the case.

Was It the Same UFO?

Thirty days later, on April 23, a six-year-old named Kim witnessed a most unusual sight. The Waterville *Morning Sentinel* reported that she and her cousins were at play in a field behind the Kennebec Mill area in Bingham. The cousins ran home to grab some more toys while Kim waited in the field for them to return. A moment later, a silver object descended into the field and landed approximately thirty feet from the child. Startled, yet fascinated by what she was witnessing, she couldn't help but just stand there and stare. She described it as a "big ball" or a "bubble" with red and green blinking lights. She actually walked up to the object, afraid but curious, and noticed a "door." She later described the UFO to a *Morning Sentinel* news reporter as "a sphere resembling a large bubble, the size of a large car, but higher" and "of a shiny metallic color, with a sort of door and window."

Without warning, things soon got scary for Kim. She saw a man inside the craft. "I saw a man in it with something on or over his head. He took it off and smiled at me.

He said something for I saw his lips move." This is when Kim took off. Once home, she tried to explain what she had seen to her mother, but her mom initially dismissed the girl's story. Days later, a family friend visited, to whom Kim retold the story. This time the mother listened and believed her daughter. The mother, a reporter, and the authorities went to the field in question and saw a scorched area of vegetation, like in John King's encounter.

Authorities now supported the little girl's story and agreed she was telling the truth as she had known it to be. Investigator Ray Fowler believed her as well and recommended the family take her to the police. An investigation ensued, but much like with King's encounter, the case was quickly dropped due to the lack of evidence. Frustrated with the outcome, the family still defended the girl's story.

The similarities to King's encounter are interesting. King first thought his UFO was an overturned car, and the little girl described a bubble with a door and window; from a distance, this could look like a common vehicle. Both incidents had reports of scorched vegetation and happened only thirty days apart. If there is a connection, I am unsure of what it would mean other than that the same UFO was traveling about Maine. But perhaps the second visit was some sort of sign of goodwill from our alien brethren. I say this because the first encounter ended violently for King, shooting at the UFO approaching him. A month later, the UFO attempted contact again by ever so lightly, and kindly, landing in a field next to an innocent little girl.

FRIGHTENING THINGS WITH ANGRY EYES

The following includes an update to my story "A Case for David Stephens," originally featured in *UFOs Over Maine: Close Encounters from the Pine Tree State.*

The Recap

Just days before Halloween, on the evening of October 27, 1975, David Stephens and Glen Gray were hanging out at their home in Norway, Maine. At approximately three o'clock in the morning, the pair heard a loud explosion from outside. I wrote previously, "The two men ran to see what had disturbed the stillness of a late fall night, but found nothing out of the ordinary. On a whim, it is told, David and Glen got into their vehicle and decided to drive toward the Lake Thompson area in Oxford. Following Route 26 for less than a mile, the men claimed that some sort of force field enveloped their car."

Once they reached the lake, they saw a bright light in an adjacent field. The light slowly rose into the air and the full extent of the light source was seen. A massive, cylinder-shaped object hovered overhead and moved toward their car. The men sped out of the area. What was to follow over the subsequent months became one of the oddest and most well-documented cases of alien abduction/men in black visitations that Maine has ever seen. It rivals the Allagash Abductions and the Loring Air Force Base incident, and was the catalyst for the Herbert Hopkins "men in black" story, since David Stephens was the patient on whom Dr. Hopkins had conducted hypnotic regression therapy.

The Update

On the evening of October 28, 1975, UFO investigator Brent Raynes received a phone call from fellow investigator Shirley Fickett about the incident in Oxford. Two hours later he was on-site and interviewed David and Glen. Brent found the men believable, but the story was intense, highly detailed, and, quite frankly, inexplicable. Brent, like myself, never shies away from a fantastic story dismissively. He listened intently and wrote down everything he could. We corresponded in June of 2017 about the incident and he said, "Word of David's experience in a small town spread like wildfire. People started looking up and seeing things, too. Some of it stars and planets, but then other incidents, who knows. A lot of people seemed to believe there was something odd going on back then."

In addition to the multi-UFO sightings occurring the night before, David and Glen also complained of odd paranormal activity in and outside of their home. During the daylight hours of the 28th, before Brent's arrival, the two men went back to the area of the abduction and observed ash falling like snow, and they could see black cubes and silver spheres flying about. Inside their home, they witnessed small black cubes floating through walls, golden wires appearing and disappearing above the television set, and an ashtray float up into the air and drop back down. David complained of unexplained knocks at the front door as well as footsteps on the roof of his home, and of a voice that said, "UFO." Afterwards, David fell into a deep sleep. Raynes said of the activity, "I had heard of similar odd elements in such cases, as well as the paranormal aspects (i.e., the ashtray episode, the voice that said UFO, etc.) and I later found a woman experiencer in Dover-Foxcroft who had 'visions' that were somewhat similar that began for her around the same time as the Oxford incident began."

Sixteen days later, Shirley Fickett visited David and Glen to conduct more interviews. After hearing about their missing time and their thoughts on possibly being abducted,

Shirley recommended hypnosis "to pull together the missing facts." She was introduced to Dr. Herbert Hopkins and he agreed to conduct the hypnotic regression sessions for free, to further his studies on the subject. The first session began on December 2, 1975, and continued through March 23, 1976, totaling eight hypnotic regression sessions. Through these sessions, David revealed having been aboard a UFO and seeing his captors. In her article for *Flying Saucer Review* about the event, Shirtley wrote that "it was soon established that a non-human being came in to join David. Although it was not human, we learned from David that it was a living being, but not of this world."

After the first session, Glen withdrew from further analysis and eventually moved out of state. David felt for his friend, realizing that the ordeal had deeply shaken him. Despite this, David kept up with the sessions. He described the beings to Shirley and Dr. Hopkins. Shirley drew a picture of one, based on his description, and David drew one as well. Shirley stated, "We learned that the skin was white, the head was shaped like a mushroom, and that it had two eyes (slanted, large, white and unblinking). The nose was small and rounded; no mouth could be observed." David pointed out that they wore long black gowns and had three fingers—webbed. They're frightening things with angry eyes. He also conveyed, while hypnotized, that samples were taken from him, which included blood, hair, and nails.

He was thoroughly examined head to toe for approximately forty-five minutes.

In January of 1976, Brent Raynes contacted longtime collaborator and psychiatrist Berthold Eric Schwarz, MD, for his take on the abduction and hypnotic sessions completed to date. Raynes recounted that "Dr. Schwarz, who was a psychiatrist, came up from Montclair, New Jersey, to investigate the Oxford case. I had called him in on the case. Dr. Hopkins was a medical doctor, but to my knowledge not a psychiatrist." Schwarz interviewed David and his family and found them to be of sound mind and body. His report stated, "There was no evidence from David's past history, or from interviews with his father and stepmother, for dishonesty, lying, falsification of or loss of memory, previous sociopathic or dissociative behavior, or of excessive interest in flying saucers, and no detailed knowledge of the Betty and Barney Hill abduction case … "

It is interesting to note that Dr. Schwarz mentioned the Betty and Barney Hill case. One week before David and Glen's encounter, the movie version of the Betty and Barney Hill story, called *The UFO Incident* (which can be viewed in full on YouTube), was televised. Robert Cahill, author of *New England's Visitors from Outer Space*, stated that David and Glen "gained national attention from many UFO investigators … but conservative UFO investigators concluded that it was more than coincidence that their adventures came only one week after a full-length movie about Betty Hill's experience was aired on national television."

For you, dear reader, this is one of those moments where you should not simply dismiss the David Stephens case just because it would be easy to. Instead, peruse the literature that has been written about the incident and consider the information I provided previously about Dr. Herbert Hopkins. You can find David's story in *Borderlands* by Mike Dash and in my first book, as well as in the fascinating related articles in *Flying Saucer Review* written by Raynes, Fickett, and Schwarz.

ALLAGASH OR BALDERDASH?

If you're a connoisseur of UFO phenomena, then you are no stranger to the work of author and UFO researcher Raymond E. Fowler. He published his first book, *UFOs: Interplanetary Visitors,* in 1974 and has since become synonymous with the Betty Andreasson abduction, which resulted in Fowler writing three books on her experiences. He's joined the ranks of researchers held in high regard, such as John Keel, J. Allen Hynek, Jerome Clark, Budd Hopkins, Jenny Randles, Linda Howe, Brent Raynes, Stanton Friedman, George Knapp, and many, many more. Currently retired from UFO investigations, Fowler now provides adult education courses in Kennebunk, Maine, that range from alien abduction to out-of-body experiences to the afterlife. He is also known for writing the definitive book on a Maine abduction tale, entitled *The Allagash Abductions: Undeniable Evidence of Alien Intervention.*

The following is an update to my story of "The Allagash Abductions," featured in *UFOs Over Maine: Close Encounters from the Pine Tree State.*

The Recap

In 1976, two years after Fowler had published his first book, four friends traveled to the Allagash Wilderness Waterway in Aroostook County. The plan was for them to have a two-week vacation of camping and fishing, but they found themselves in the throes of an otherworldly experience, the events of which affected the four men for a lifetime. I wrote about their experiences in my first book: "In the summer of 1976, four men ventured north from their college in Massachusetts to the beautifully pristine Allagash Wilderness Waterway in Northern Maine for a long trip of fishing, camping, and living off the land." The four friends—Chuck Rak, Charlie Foltz, and identical twin brothers Jack and Jim Weiner—spotted a UFO on the second night of their trip, along with other witnesses. A few nights later, while canoeing on Eagle Lake, they spotted another UFO and later claimed that a CE-4 (alien abduction) took place. Chuck Rak described this UFO as follows: "I could see a fluid pulsating over the face of the object as it changed color from red to green to yellow-white." After they witnessed the UFO, the men finished with their fishing and headed back to shore. But when they arrived, the large fire they had built was reduced to embers, suggesting that they had been gone much longer than originally thought. Hours, in fact.

Years after the incident, with vague memories of the abductions, Jim Weiner attended a UFO conference and met Ray Fowler. Weiner disclosed having had seizures and as a result seeing visions of aliens surrounding his bed. He explained his UFO sighting years earlier, and Fowler agreed to help Jim and the others. Hypnosis sessions were set up, and the friends were surprised to learn about their abduction experiences while on the lake. As I then explain in my first book, "It was revealed that the four abductees had somehow been transported to the UFO from their canoes. It is assumed that a beam of light, which was witnessed by the men, was how this transportation occurred. Jim stated during a hypnosis session, *the beam-it's going to get us! It's right there, right behind us. I know there's no use. It's no use paddling. The beam! It's got us! It's there. We're in it!* Once on board the unidentified vessel, the men succumbed to some sort of mind control or manipulation by very odd-looking beings. Forced to remove all their clothing, the four friends were then led to a plastic seating area. This is where a lot of the preliminary examinations took place. The gentlemen were poked and prodded … "

Fowler published his book about the men's experience in 1993, and their story was featured on the *Joan Rivers Show* and on an episode of *Unsolved Mysteries.*

The Update (Dissonance)

As the decades went by, Chuck Rak began to distance himself from the other abductees. He no longer made appearances at conventions, and stopped talking with his old friends all together. In 2016, the *Fiddlehead Focus* newspaper out of Madawaska, Maine, interviewed Chuck in an article titled "Subject of 1976 UFO Incident Casts Doubt on 'Allagash Abductions.'" Chuck stated, "The reason I supported the story at first is because I wanted to make money. We were compelled to stay together, all speculating that this thing could go into the millions of dollars for each of us, we made very little." Jim, Jack, and Charlie disagreed with Chuck's statement, and it became clear that some sort of falling out had occurred. Chuck did admit to the newspaper that he did see UFOs while on their trip, but stated, "I don't call it a hoax, just brilliant storytelling. It's not the truth, but I have to admire the storytelling ability of these guys."

One of the most interesting facets of the story is the purported "missing time" suggested by the large fire the men had built before leaving shore. They started the fire to help them navigate back to their campsite after they were done fishing. As discussed previously, they were gone for so long that only embers remained. Chuck again punched holes in the abduction story when he told the interviewer, "It certainly was a big fire, I agree with that. Those logs were maybe three inches. Some of them could have been almost three and a half inches, that's the biggest they could have been; and most of them were smaller, and as such in that condition those pieces of wood would have burned off very quickly."

This statement weighs heavily in the validity of the abduction scenario. It's the crux, if you will, of the missing time. The abduction story all starts with the fire. The newspaper also reached out to Charlie Foltz, who responded to this claim by stating, "Some of the wood we put on there was about the diameter of my leg. I would say at least a good 10 inches in diameter easily."

Chuck also brought up drug usage and explained to the interviewer that all of them were "stoned" during their trip. "Yeah, we were definitely stoned when we went out on the lake just before we got that sighting." Wow! Another devastating blow to the story, putting the entire event into question. Charlie vehemently denied the accusation, however, and stated, "No. We bought an eight-pack of beer in Millinocket when we bought all of our supplies for the canoe trip. We each had one beer at Telos Landing the very first night and we each had one beer at Fort Kent the last day of our canoe trip. We carried those eight bottles in and we carried those eight bottles back out." He also spoke out against Chuck's character and described him as a guy with a "violent temper who has been banned from some UFO conventions. We definitely steer clear of him because the guy is a loose cannon and a mental disaster area."

With all of this back and forth, how can one discern what really happened? Realistically, it's in your hands. Who do you choose to believe? Do you even believe in alien abduction at all? I have an opinion, based on my research of the case. It is also based on my immense respect for Ray Fowler, and for the way Jim, Jack, and Charlie have conducted themselves throughout the years in interviews and conventions. Simply, I believe them.

The remaining friends insist that they were the ones who distanced themselves from Chuck, and they have continued to stand by their story. The event has changed the men profoundly, both emotionally and physically. They want to continue to share their story to help others cope with their own experiences. In a 2013 interview with the *Bangor Daily News,* Jim Weiner reinforced how the encounter continued to impact their lives: "This is not a club you want to be a member of. You want answers. You don't get it from government, religion ... it leads you on a quest. It forced me to revisit my outlook about the world and my community. It changes who you are. You are not the same after this."

The Allagash Abductions played a large role in bringing me into the field of ufology. I watched the *Unsolved Mysteries* program as a child and was fascinated by their story. Having had my own UFO experience at five years old (you can read about it in my first book), I couldn't believe that others in Maine had had experiences as well. I had read about witnesses from other states and countries, but nothing hit home as much as this landmark case. Still, despite my bias, I always and wholeheartedly welcome you to form your own opinion.

CONCLUSION

If you'll indulge me for a moment, I'm going to end this book with a question. *Why does any of this matter?* A lot has been discussed in this writing. Themes about perception and belief, and stories about hard-to-believe abductions, men in black, military encounters, and more. My question is not rhetorical. Why do you think it matters? Why would someone like myself, or Erik or Valerie, spend so much time on such a topic? Why did you pick up this book? If you're one of my friends, maybe it's because you know me. But for believers, it's something different, isn't it? It can be hard to explain, but realistically, it's simple. We believe, *and* we enjoy reading, hearing, and watching stories about unidentified flying objects.

Believers in the paranormal are truly attuned to their surroundings. What is unnoticeable to one is apparent to another. I sky-watch constantly; my friend does not. I am more apt to see something unexplainable; however, do I run the risk of misidentification? I like to call this the "Mulder Effect," based on the Fox Mulder character in *The X-Files*. Mulder is the type of person who wants to believe so badly, every sound in an old house is a ghost, every snap in the woods a Sasquatch, and every light in the sky a UFO.

If my father were to tell me that he saw a UFO, I would stop whatever it was I was doing and listen thoroughly. I would because I know him and his beliefs (he's a skeptic all day, for the record). If I saw a video on SecureTeam10's YouTube page ... well, based on their previous video choices, I would have a harder time believing it.

So, what are your thoughts about my opinions and the stories shared in this book, including my own encounters? Do I have credibility with you? I would hope so, but you don't have too much to base it on other than the sincerity with which I write and the effort put forth in my research, investigations, and interviews. Case in point—literally this evening (May 10, 2017, at 7:15 p.m.), I took a break from writing to have a cigarette outside. As I stood there, I observed an amber light high in the sky. I assumed it was Venus. Not a minute later, I looked back and it was gone. Planets do not disappear; well, except for Pluto (lol). Maybe I looked too briefly and it was a plane, although I was sure it had no blinking lights.

Regardless, I perceived something unique. Quite literally, an unidentified flying object.

Perception played a major role in how I have written these stories *and* how you have read these stories. We all have formed our own opinions, biases, and generalities. For me, I have had firsthand conversations with some of the witnesses in this book, and that alone can play a dramatic role in shaping my opinion of a perceived event. I have shared encounters from folks from all levels of society who believe they perceived something otherworldly. Doctors, policemen, retirees, lobstermen, trappers, toddlers, and everyone in between. If perception is reality, then we already know that we are not alone. Right?

Recently I spoke with a twenty-year military veteran who told me, "Well, I haven't seen anything weird in the skies yet. But to think we're alone in the universe would be ridiculous." What we have here is an example of a non-event—one man's opinion. We call that the "gray area." I'm sure most of us (this author and you readers) fall into this category. I say this because even though I am a "believer," there are some stories that I simply do not believe. Remember "sans bias"? How do we get there from here?

Especially with UFOs. It's a tough question due to the vast amount of fakery with images, videos, and stories. Stan Romanek is a household name amongst ufologists, but ask if we believe his story? Well, the images and videos that he's produced are truly hard to swallow. The documentary

Extraordinary: The Stan Romanek Story is compelling, and well-made, but did it turn me into a believer of Romanek's stories? No. So, how do we get to *actual reality* instead of just perception? Part of the answer may be "shared perceptions."

I spoke with another gentleman who told me of an encounter he had at five years old. In 1978, he was leaving a local grocery store with his grandmother in South Portland, Maine. (It is now the area where Staples is located near the Jetport.) As the young boy waited for his grandmother to load their car with grocery bags, he noticed a peculiar object in the sky. It hovered low over the airport; he described it as "gray, egg shaped, and as big as a tractor-trailer truck." He remembered minute details of it and told me it "had a matte finish, not shiny at all." He brought it to his grandmother's attention, but she dismissed him. After insisting, she finally looked up, but it was gone. The boy never took his eyes off the oddity and watched as it hid behind a cloud. It never reappeared.

Later that same year, this gentleman's brother, who was twelve at the time, had an interesting encounter of his own. A friend told him that a UFO had landed right behind Merrill's Seafood on Forest Avenue in Portland, Maine. After school, the boys went to check out where it had supposedly landed, and they were rather surprised to find scorch marks on the ground! (The back parking lot of Merrill's was unpaved at the time.) Witnesses told them that the UFO slowed, landed in the area, and stayed for a moment, and when it took off, all electrical power in the immediate vicinity went out. Fascinated by his brother's story, he called Merrill's Seafood some thirty-five years later to inquire about the event. He was not given any additional information, but sure enough he had had a shared perception with his brother. It was at different times, but they believed in similarly themed events. This can be easy to ignore or dismiss, but sharing a belief with someone can breed love, bonds, worship (shared religious beliefs), etc.

My girlfriend and I experienced our own shared perception in November 2016. We were sitting out on our deck on a particularly warmer-than-normal evening for that time of year. It was about 9:00 p.m. when a light in the sky caught my attention. I turned for a better look and observed two bright, low-altitude lights in the sky, one above the other, at an angle. "What do you think that is?" I said as I pointed toward the sky. To view it more clearly, she had to get up and move closer to my vantage point to see it. She was a bit dumbfounded and said, "That's weird." Just then, we both observed the two lights retreat backwards and fade out. Certainly odd, and technically an unidentified flying object, but more importantly, a shared perception.

Maybe what is needed to truly study this type of phenomenon is to conduct group investigations so that shared perceptions are more recognizable. This did occur at the Skinwalker Ranch, when NIDSci had multiple scientists and doctors investigate in groups. They had shared perceptions of Sasquatch, UFOs, and other types of paranormal activity. I think it's a great approach to start with. But realistically, it's a needle's point beginning of where to go with ufology.

We've covered a lot in this writing. I have presented stories as factually as possible for you. Some have been firsthand accounts from witnesses that I personally interviewed; others reached out to me via Facebook or email, and some were sent to me from MUFON's Valerie Schultz. Between Erik Cooley and I, we found hundreds of unique stories in newspapers, books, and on the internet. In the introduction to this book, I mentioned how difficult it was to pick which stories to share. Some just did not have enough information to write about fully, while some great stories could not be shared due to permission or privacy. On the other hand, some stories were so vast that they really could garner their own book—for example, ones from Shalel Way, the Stratton area, Wilhelm Reich, and more. The stories that I did not write about can be easily found at MUFON, at NUFORC, and in articles, books, essays, and websites such as *UFO Casebook* and *AP Magazine* (just to name a couple; there are literally thousands). Some other authors who have written Maine UFO stories include Jenny Randles, Stanton Friedman, Loren Coleman, B. J. Booth, Robert Cahill, Jerome Clark, and Roger Marsh.

When you're looking up at the sky, remember to "look into" as well. There are so many stories just waiting to be uncovered!

BIBLIOGRAPHY

"1600-1649 UFO & Alien Sightings." Think About It-Docs: UFO & Alien Sightings by Date & Location. http://www.thinkaboutitdocs.com/1600-1649-ufo-alien-sightings/.

"Alien Abductions." Crystalinks: Metaphysics and Science website, n.d. http://www.crystalinks.com/abduction.html.

"Alien Abduction: Hoax or Reality?" *World Mysteries Blog*, December 12, 2012. http://blog.world-mysteries.com/science/alien-abduction-hoax-or-reality/.

Austin, Jon. "Exclusive UFO Sensation: Could Amazing Footage Be First Video Proof of Mysterious TR-3B." *Express: Home of the Daily and Sunday Express,* June 14, 2016. http://www.express.co.uk/news/weird/679732/exclusive-ufo-sensation-could-amazing-footage-be-first-video-proof-of-mysterious-TR-3B.

Aviation Safety Network. "ASN Aircraft Accident Lockheed P-3B-75-LO Orion 152757 Poland, ME," 1978. https://aviation-safety.net/database/record.php?id=19780922-0.

"Bay of Fundy Ship UFO Seen in 1796." *The Evening News* (Newburgh, NY), November 30, 1967. Google News. https://news.google.com/newspapers?nid=1982&dat=19671130&id=QBpgAAAAIBAJ&sjid=tm0NAAAAIBAJ&pg=6523,5961349&hl=en.

Bechtel, Leland. "UFO the Size of a 747." *MUFON UFO Journal,* no. 198 (October 10, 1984): 14–15. doi:Disclosure Project.

"Bingham Girl Says She Observed UFO." *The Morning Sentinel* (Waterville, ME), May 6, 1966.

BLT Research Team, Inc. USA Crop Circles, 2009. http://www.bltresearch.com/usacropcircles/?page_id=155.

Blum, Howard. *I Pledge Allegiance: The True Story of the Walkers: An American Spy Family.* New York: Simon & Schuster, 1987.

Booth, B. J. *UFOs Caught on Film: Amazing Evidence of Alien Visitors to Earth*. Newton Abbot, UK: F & W Media, 2012.

Braxton, Eugene. *America's Mystic Solves Near-Death Riddle*. Bloomington, IN: Archway Publishing, 2014.

Brogan, Beth. "Mystery Boom Befuddles Maine Authorities." *Bangor Daily News*, April 10, 2017.

Bullard, Thomas E. *UFO Abductions: The Measure of a Mystery*. Bloomington, IN: Fund for UFO Research, 1987.

Cahill, Robert Ellis. *New England's Visitors from Outer Space*. 3rd ed. Peabody, MA: Chandler-Smith Publishing House, 1985.

Clark, Jerome, and Loren Coleman. *Creatures of the Goblin World*. New York: Clark Publishing, 1984.

———. *The Unidentified & Creatures of the Outer Edge: The Early Works of Jerome Clark and Loren Coleman*. New York: Anomalist Books, 2006.

"Close Encounters." The Black Vault, March 30, 2006. http://www.theblackvault.com/wiki/index.php /Close_encounter.

Coleman, Loren. *Mothman and Other Curious Encounters*. 3rd ed. New York: Paraview Press, 2002.

Crawford, John. "The Strange Lights of Stratton." *Boston Phoenix*, February 22, 2012.

Cummings, Abraham. *Immortality Proved by the Testimony of Sense: In Which is Contemplated the Doctrine of Spectres and the Existence of a Particular Spectre Addressed to the Candor of this Enlightened Age.* Portland, ME: J. L Lovell, 1859.

Dash, Mike. *Borderlands: The Ultimate Exploration of the Unknown.* Woodstock, NY: Overlook Press, 1999.

Dauphinee, Dave. "Cold War Relics." Cold War Relics— Dow AFB. http://coldwarrelics.com/dow_afb, accessed 2009 (site discontinued).

David, Leonard. "CIA About UFOs of the 1950s and '60s: 'It Was Us.'" Space.com, January 14, 2015. http://www .space.com/28256-ufo-sightings-cia-u2-aircraft.html.

Delonge, Tom, and A. J. Hartley. *Sekret Machines Book 1: Chasing Shadows.* Encinitas, CA: To the Stars, Inc., 2016.

Devoe, Stephen. "UFO at Shaker Village in Gray, Maine." UF-Devoe, 2004. http://ghostologee.ipower.com /uf-devoe.htm.

Ducasse, Curt John. *Paranormal Phenomena, Science, and Life After Death (Parapsychological Monographs No. 8).* New York: Parapsychology Foundation, 1969.

"Family with Many Troubles at Center of Espionage Case." *The New York Times*, June 10, 1985.

Fawcett, Lawrence, and Barry J. Greenwood. *The UFO Cover-Up: What the Government Won't Say*. New York: Simon & Schuster/Fireside, 1992.

Fickett, Shirley M. "The Maine UFO Encounter: Investigating Under Hypnosis." *Flying Saucer Review* 22, no. 2 (July 1976): 14–17.

FitzGerald, Michael. *Alien Arrival: Salvation or Destruction*. Atglen, PA: Schiffer Publishing, Ltd., 2014.

Fluet, M. R. *Our Brothers in the Skies: The Hidden Truth Revealed*. Bloomington, IN: AuthorHouse, 2009.

Fowler, Raymond E. *The Allagash Abductions: Undeniable Evidence of Alien Intervention*. Columbus, NC: Wild Flower Press, 2005.

———. *UFOs: Interplanetary Visitors: A UFO Investigator Reports on the Facts, Fables, and Fantasies of the Flying Saucer Conspiracy*. San Jose: Authors Choice Press, 2001.

Godfrey, Linda S. *Real Wolfmen: True Encounters in Modern America*. New York: Tarcher/Penguin, 2012.

Grard, Larry. "They Saw Strange Lights in the Sky." *The Morning Sentinel* (Waterville, ME), February 23, 2007.

Gratzer, Walter. *The Undergrowth of Science: Delusion, Self-Deception and Human Frailty*. Oxford: Oxford University Press, 2000.

Greenwood, Barry, and Larry Fawcett. "Intrusions at Loring AFB—1975." NICAP, May 30, 2007. http://www.nicap.org/articles/CI-Loring.htm.

Greer, Steven M. "The CE-5 Initiative." Transcript from speech, April 8, 1995. Sirius Disclosure. http://siriusdisclosure.com/wp-content/uploads/2012/12/CE-5-Initiative-Transcript.pdf.

Hargrove, Rose. "Post Abduction Syndrome (PAS): Description of an Emerging Syndrome," February 14, 2000. http://aliensandchildren.org/post_abduction_syn.htm.

Hastings, Robert. "UFO Sightings at ICBM sites and nuclear Weapons Storage Areas." NICAP, 2006. https://www.nicap.org/babylon/missile_incidents.htm

———. "UFO Sightings by Air Policemen at Loring AFB, Maine, in the 1960s." The UFO Chronicles, March 18, 2012. http://www.theufochronicles.com/2013/03/ufo-sightings-by-air-policemen-at.html.

Hopkins, Budd, David M. Jacobs, and Ron Westrum. *Unusual Personal Experiences: An Analysis of the Data from Three Major Surveys Conducted by the Roper Organization*. Las Vegas: Bigelow Holding Corporation, 1992.

Hopkins, Howard. "More MIB Weirdery." Dark Bits, January 23, 2008. https://web.archive.org/web/20080723185406/http://howardhopkins.blogspot.com/2008/01/more-mib-weirdery.html.

———. "The Truth About a Man in Black." Dark Bits, January 13, 2008. https://web.archive.org/web/20080524015603/http://howardhopkins.blogspot.com/2008/01/truth-about-man-in-black.html.

Hufford, David J. Foreword to *Wonders in the Sky: Unexplained Aerial Objects from Antiquity to Modern Times* by Jacques Vallee and Chris Aubeck. New York: Tarcher/Penguin, 2010.

Hynek, J. Allen. *The UFO Experience: A Scientific Inquiry.* New York: Ballantine Books, 1977.

Hyre, Mary. "Winged, Red-Eyed 'Thing' Chases Point Couples Across Countryside." *The Athens Messenger*, November 16, 1966.

Independent Crop Circle Researchers' Association. "Reported Crop Circles for the State of Maine," 2011. http://www.iccra.org/bystate/Maine/ICCRA%20-%20ME%20-%20Turner,%20Androscoggin%20County%20(1959).htm

IntCat 1955 list. IntCat: International Catalog of Close Encounters and Entity Reports. http://intcat.blogspot.com/2012/08/intcat-1955.html.

IntCat 1966, Jan-June list. IntCat: International Catalog of Close Encounters and Entity Reports. http://intcat .blogspot.com/2012/09/intcat-1966-jan-june.html.

Jacobs, David M. *Secret Life: Firsthand Documented Accounts of UFO Abductions.* New York: Simon & Shuster/Fireside, 1993.

Johndro, Maureen. "Loring Air Force Base History." Loring Military Heritage Center, n.d. http://www .loringmilitaryheritagecenter.com/loring-history.html.

Keel, John A. *The Mothman Prophecies.* New York: Tor, 2002.

LaFraniere, Sharon, and Ruth Marcus. "Spy Tip Followed Tarot Cards Ex-Wife." *Washington Post,* June 6, 1985.

Lang, Nico. "11 Totally Insane Scientific Theories People Used to Believe Were True." Thought Catalog, October 7, 2013. http://thoughtcatalog.com/nico -lang/2013/10/11-totally-insane-scientific-theories -people-used-to-believe-were-true/.

Lovell-Keely, Molly. "Paranormal Class Ok'd for Adult Ed." *Kennebunk Post,* March 4, 2016. http://post .mainelymediallc.com/news/2016-03-04/Community /Paranormal_class_OKd_for_Adult_Ed.html.

MacIsaac, Tara. "Medieval Woodcut Shows UFO Battle Over Nuremberg Germany, 1561?" The Epoch Times, updated March 29, 2015. https://www.theepochtimes .com/medieval-woodcut-seems-to-describe-ufo-battle-over-nuremburg-germany-1561_735667.html.

Mack, John E. *Abduction: Human Encounters with Aliens.* New York: Charles Scribner's Sons, 1994.

Marsh, Roger. "Maine Witness Describes Close Encounter with Triangle UFO." OpenMinds. April 10, 2017. http://www.openminds.tv/maine-witness-describes -close-encounter-with-triangle-ufo/39948.

McLeod, S. A. "Visual Perception Theory." Simply Psychology, 2007. http://www.simplypsychology.org /perception-theories.html.

"Folklore." Merriam-Webster.com. Accessed April 13, 2018. https://www.merriam-webster.com/dictionary /folklore.

Montgomery, Ruth. *Strangers Among Us.* Fawcett Crest, New York: 1982.

"More Witnesses Report Seeing Bright-Colored County Fireball." *Bangor Daily News*, January 30, 1998.

MUFON (Mutual UFO Network). http://www.mufon .com/.

MUFON Search Database. http://www.mufon.com/search
-database---comp.html.

NASA. "Earth Songs." NASA Science Mission
Directorate. https://science.nasa.gov/science-news
/science-at-nasa/2001/ast19jan_1.

Naisbitt, Michael. "Defining a Close Encounter." E.T.
Observer, May 21, 2012. http://etobserver.blogspot
.com/2012/05/defining-close-encounter.html.

NIDSci (National Institute for Discovery Science).
Discovery Science articles list. http://www.nidsci.org
/discovery-science/.

NICAP (National Investigations Committee of Aerial
Phenomena). "Press Spotlight." *The UFO Investigator* 3,
no. 6 (February 1966): 1–2.

"Obituary: Prentiss Godfrey." *Bangor Daily News*, March
17, 2011.

Parsons, Jeff. "Multiple Lights Appear and Disappear
in Sky Over Buxton, Maine (Video)." SOTT: Signs
of the Times, December 20, 2016. https://sott.net/
article/337697-Multiple-lights-appear-and-disappear
-in-sky-over-Buxton-Maine-VIDEO.

"Perception." Dictionary.com Unabridged. Random House,
Inc. Accessed April 18, 2018. http://www.dictionary
.com/browse/perception.

Pfeifer, Ken. "Alien Abduction in Maine." World
UFO Photos and News, October 2010. http://
worldufophotosandnews.org/?p=1233.

———. "Strange Objects Witnessed Over Maine." World
UFO Photos and News, March 16, 2012. http://
worldufophotosandnews.org/?p=2312.

Pierce, Kathleen. "Portland 'Alien Abduction' Conference
Discusses Stories, Truth of Close Encounters." *Bangor
Daily News*, September 8, 2013.

Potila, Jessica. "Subject of 1976 UFO Incident Casts
Doubt on 'Allagash Abductions.'" Fiddlehead Focus,
September 10, 2016. http://fiddleheadfocus
.com/2016/09/10/news/community/top-stories
/subject-of-1976-ufo-incident-casts-doubt-on
-allagash-abductions/.

Project Blue Book. Presque Isle Air Force Base, Case
29/1455Z, Rep. No. 29/1455Z. January 1953.

Quimby, Beth. "UFO Believers Share Close
Encounters." *Portland Press Herald*, September 8, 2012.
https://www.pressherald.com/2012/09/08/speakers
-talk-about-their-encounters-with-extraterrestrials/.

Raynes, Brent M. "Reality Checking." AP Magazine,
April 2014. http://apmagazine.info/index
.php?option=com_content&view=article&id=528%3A
reality-checking-august-2025&catid=2&Itemid=194.

———. "The Twilight Side of a UFO Encounter." *Flying Saucer Review* 22, no. 2 (July 1976): 11–13.

"Reader Recounts 1982 UFO Encounter in Maine." UFO Casebook, 2008. http://www.ufocasebook .com/2008c/1982eliotmaine.html.

Reich, Wilhelm. *Contact with Space: Oranur Second Report 1951-1956.* Cream Ridge, NJ: Core Pilot Press, 1957.

Rense, Jeff. "Maine UFO Researcher Shirley Fickett Passes." Obituary from *Portland Press Herald*, February 3, 2005. http://rense.com/general62/shirley.htm.

Ridge, Francis. "The 1973 UFO Chronology: A Worldwide Wave." NICAP, April 15, 2007. http://www.nicap.org /chronos/1973fullrep.htm.

"Rocket Launch Prompts Calls of Strange Lights in Sky." CNN, September 20, 2009. http://www.cnn.com/2009 /US/09/20/strange.lights/index.html.

Rojas, Alejandro. "Angel Hair Falling from the Heavens or UFOs?" OpenMinds, November 12, 2010. http://www .openminds.tv/angel-hair-ufos/6513.

———. "UFO Researcher Offers Adult Education Classes on the Paranormal." OpenMinds, June 3, 2014. http:// www.openminds.tv/ufo-researcher-offers-adult -education-classes-paranormal/28035.

Rosales, Albert. "Humanoids Reports: 1997–2007."
No. 164, 2001, pgs. 532–33. http://studylib.net/
doc/8052020/humanoids-reports-1997-2007.doc.

"The Sad Truth Behind an MIB Story." *Magonia Review of
Books*, February 27, 2009. http://pelicanist.blogspot
.com/2009/02/sad-truth-behind-mib-story.html.

Sarnacki, Aislinn. "Is Maine Home to the First
Documented Haunting in the US?" *Bangor Daily
News*, October 30, 2015.

"Saucer-type 'ship' with multi-colored lights, landed in
yard." UFO Evidence, 2005. http://www.ufoevidence
.org/Cases/case332.htm.

Schwarz, Berthold E. "The Man-in-Black Syndrome."
Flying Saucer Review 23, no. 4 (1978): 9–14.

———. "Psychiatric-Paranormal Aspects of the Maine
Encounter." *Flying Saucer Review* 22, no. 2 (July 1976):
18–22.

———. *UFO Dynamics: Psychiatric and Psychic Dimensions
of the UFO Syndrome.* Moore Haven, FL: Rainbow
Books, 1983.

Seavey, Wendell. *Working the Sea: Misadventures, Ghost
Stories, and Life Lessons from a Maine Lobsterman.*
Berkeley, CA: North Atlantic Books, 2010.

Sharaf, Myron. *Fury on Earth: A Biography of Wilhelm Reich*. New York: Da Capo Press, 1994.

"Sighting Reports Previous to 1990: Man Recalls Abduction Experience." UFOs Northwest. http://www.ufosnw .com/sighting_reports/older/newgloucesterme1973 /newgloucesterme1973.htm.

Slevik, Nomar. *UFOs Over Maine: Close Encounters from the Pine Tree State*. Atglen, PA: Schiffer Publishing, Ltd., 2014.

SOBEPS (Belgian Society for the Study of Space Phenomena). *Vague d'OVNI sur la Belgique: Un Dossier Exceptionnel*. Brussels: SOBEPS, 1991.

Souliere, Michelle. "The Latest Maine UFO Sighting: Orrington." *Strange Maine*, June 16, 2015. http:// strangemaine.blogspot.com/2015/06/the-latest-maine -ufo-sighting-orrington.html.

Stephens, Kay. "More of the Story Behind the Lobsterman and the UFO." *PenBay Pilot*, July 21, 2015. http://www.penbaypilot.com/article /more-story-behind-lobsterman-and-ufo/56528.

Stevens, C. J. *The Supernatural Side of Maine*. Phillips, ME: John Wade, 2002.

Stokes, Hal. "Diary Describes UFO Seen In 1808." *Courier-Freeman* (Potsdam, NY), March 28, 1978.

Strickler, Lon. "Amazing Photo! UFO Bright Cone of Light—Acadia National Park, Maine." Phantoms & Monsters, September 20, 2009. http://www.phantomsandmonsters.com/2009/09/amazing-photo-ufo-bright-cone-of-light.html.

———. "Daily 2 Cents: Amazing UFO Over Steuben, Maine—World Collapse by 2040?—Mermaid Sightings Off Queensland Coast." Phantoms & Monsters, June 23, 2015. http://www.phantomsandmonsters.com/2015/06/daily-2-cents-amazing-ufo-over-steuben.html.

"Tote Road, Maine Sightings." UFO Casebook, January 6, 2011. http://www.ufocasebook.com/2011/1968toteroadsightings.html.

"TR-3B." Dark Government, n.d. http://www.darkgovernment.com/news/tr-3b/.

Trainor, Joseph, ed. "Shirley Fickett, Maine's 'First Lady of Ufology,' Dead at Age 82." UFO Roundup 10, no. 6 (February 9, 2005). http://www.ufoinfo.com/roundup/v10/rnd1006.shtml.

"Two Low Flying Triangles Reported Over Maine." MUFON, n.d. http://www.mufon.com/feed-972277/two-low-flying-triangles-reported-over-maine.

"UFO Forming Crop Circle Best Video." Tanvir Ahmed, uploader. YouTube video, 5:16. May 1, 2008. https://www.youtube.com/watch?v=9SJvVW8s_Oc.

"UFO Report." UFO Report, March 22, 2014. http://www.nicap.org/530129presqueisle_dir.htm.

"UFO Sighting in Union, Maine on May 17, 1981." UFO Stalker. http://www.ufostalker.com/event/54993.

"UFO Sighting in Windham." UFO Hunters, n.d. http://www.ufo-hunters.com/sightings/search/51969a6b83c78d384ec2cc82/UFO%20Sighting%20in%20Windham,%20Maine%20(United%20States)%20on%20Sunday%2030%20June%201968.

"UFO with Blue Lights Snapped in Steuben." *Wakonda 666*, June 23, 2015. http://wakonda666.blogspot.com/2015/06/ufo-with-blue-lights-snapped-in-steuben.html.

Vallee, Jacques. "Five Arguments Against the Extraterrestrial Origin of Unidentified Flying Objects." *Journal of Scientific Exploration* 4, no. 1 (1990): 105–17.

Vallee, Jacques, and Chris Aubeck. *Wonders in the Sky: Unexplained Aerial Objects from Antiquity to Modern Times*. New York: Tarcher/Penguin, 2010.

Varney, Geo J. "History of Strong, Maine." Ray's Place: Explore New England's Past, n.d. http://history.rays -place.com/me/strong-me.htm.

Wessely, Christina. "Cosmic Ice Theory—Science, Fiction and the Public, 1894-1945." Max Planck Institute for the History of Science, 2006. https:// www.mpiwg-berlin.mpg.de/research/projects/ DeptIII-ChristinaWessely-Welteislehre/.

Williams, Maureen. "Object in Sky Upsets Orrington Woman." *Bangor Daily News*, June 15, 1978.

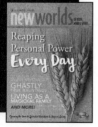